W9-CLQ-399

ADVANCE PRAISE FOR *YOUR FAMILY COMPASS*

What Jenny Hanlon does remarkably well is weave together
relevant theory and research with case studies, practical activities,
and questions that allow parents to create a family compass
unique to their own values. Her strengths-based approach offers
a refreshing and realistic understanding of behavior, without
blaming the child or making the adult feel incompetent.

—CHRISTINE HURLEY, PhD.,
LICENSED SCHOOL PSYCHOLOGIST

Your Family Compass gives parents confidence in the decisions
they make. Jenny Hanlon's easy-to-use tools help parents
support their children's needs in deliberate and loving ways. I
recommend this helpful and inspiring book for families at any
stage of development!

—ARBA-DELLA BECK, MSW , PRESIDENT, FAMILYMEANS

Jenny Hanlon successfully makes child development research
and child psychology principles accessible and useful—a truly
wonderful guide for thoughtful parents.

—NANCY JONES, M.S., FOUNDER AND EXECUTIVE DIRECTOR OF
THE CHILDREN'S FARM SCHOOL

your *family* Compass

A Parenting Guide for the Journey

Jenny Hanlon

BEAVER'S
POND
PRESS

YOUR FAMILY COMPASS © copyright 2012 by Jenny Hanlon.
All rights reserved. No part of this book may be reproduced in any form
whatsoever, by photography or xerography or by any other means, by
broadcast or transmission, by translation into any kind of language, nor by
recording electronically or otherwise, without permission in writing from
the author, except by a reviewer, who may quote brief passages in critical
articles or reviews.

ISBN 13: 978-1-59298-489-4

Library of Congress Catalog Number: 2012908585

Printed in the United States of America

First Printing: 2012

16   15   14   13   12   5   4   3   2   1

Cover design by Amanda Hanlon of ADH Studio, LLC.
Interior design and typesetting by James Monroe Design, LLC.
Cover and author photo by LeAnne Schmidt
Indexer: April Michelle Davis, Editorial Inspirations

BEAVER'S
POND
PRESS

Beaver's Pond Press, Inc.
7108 Ohms Lane
Edina, MN 55439–2129
(952) 829-8818
www.BeaversPondPress.com

To order, visit www.BeaversPondBooks.com
or call (800) 901-3480. Reseller discounts available.

To my parents, Chuck and Donna McGinley,
for always encouraging me to follow my dreams,
To my husband, Jason, for always supporting my dreams, and
To my children, Ian and Maya, for showing me that
my dreams can come true.

CONTENTS

SECTION ONE: GOALS

CHAPTER ONE

SECTION TWO: UNDERSTANDING

CHAPTER TWO

CHAPTER THREE

SECTION THREE: INDEPENDENCE

SECTION FOUR: DISCUSSIONS

SECTION FIVE: ENJOYMENT

CHAPTER TEN
Are We Actually Supposed to Enjoy This Journey? 207

FOREWORD

These days, when we travel almost any road, we can check a GPS in our car or on our smart phone to figure out exactly where we are and how to get to where we want to be. If only there were such a clear and helpful tool to help us travel the road of parenting!

Unfortunately, there is no GPS of parenting to tell us where we are and point us toward where we want to go. But family educator Jenny Hanlon has taken on the somewhat daunting task of developing what she has dubbed *Your Family Compass*, a thoughtful guidebook to help moms and dads determine the direction they want to travel as parents—that is, the kinds of values they want for themselves and their children and the goals they want to attain while nurturing and guiding their children from infancy toward a healthy, happy, productive adulthood.

Drawing on theory and research about stages of child development, individual differences in children's behaviors and personalities, and the advantages and disadvantages of different popular parenting techniques, Hanlon offers a variety of real-life examples and poses reflective questions to help parents understand the challenges they are bound to encounter and to devise effective, developmentally sound ways to move their child and themselves through the inevitable rough spots.

Your Family Compass is not for the parent who is looking for a quick fix, although certainly many of the practical tips may lead relatively quickly to improvement in a child's behavior and a calmer, happier family. But this guidebook is written for the thoughtful, reflective parent who wants to know not only what to do, but also why to do it—the parent who wants to consider the purpose and meaning of child behavior at any given age and the long-term impact of different parenting practices. This guidebook is likely to spur eager learners on to seek even more and deeper information about some of the developmental theories the author introduces.

Most of all, this guidebook is grounded in the understanding that our job as parents is not to simply find peace in the moment, but rather to use each ordinary situation or challenge to help our children build the skills that will serve them throughout their lives—from a toddler's choice of whether to wear the red shirt or the blue shirt to a teen's ability to say no when pressured to do something unhealthy or unwise.

My daughter Erin (cohost of our weekly parenting show, *Mom Enough*) often says our job as parents is to put ourselves out of a job. *Your Family Compass* will help parents do just that. Certainly our love and support is still important to our children even when they are adults. But if we have been "mom enough" or "dad enough" to our children—if we keep our eye on our long-term goals and stay vigilant to be sure we are headed in the right direction—our sons and daughters will arrive at adulthood with the motivation, confidence, competence, and compassion to live life to the fullest, with respect for themselves and others. What more could we want as parents?

—**Marti Erickson, PhD,**
director emerita, Harris Training Programs,
University of Minnesota, cohost of
Mom Enough (www.momenough.com)

INTRODUCTION

Life happens to us whether we want it to or not. We can't control every situation that comes our way. Sometimes we encounter unexpected twists and turns throughout our journey and find ourselves looking for guidance to get back on track. Unfortunately, we're not always sure where "back" is, or even what it might look like.

Our family recently took a trip to visit the coast of California and Oregon for a wedding. Our first flight went off without a hitch: the plane was on schedule, the kids had time to do their homework while I wrote, and we had a smooth landing. I thought to myself, "This is going well." As we boarded the plane again after a short layover in Denver, we were told we needed to deplane, as there was a delay due to poor weather in San Francisco. This seemed minor, but the delay kept getting longer. We finally boarded the plane two hours later than we had planned, and even though we were agitated, we tried to stay positive. We were still excited for the rest of our adventures. However, we weren't viewing the flight as part of this adventure. Perhaps next time we will.

After landing and getting our rental car, we headed toward Oakland, where we were staying for the night. Unfortunately, we ran into the traffic of those leaving the 49ers game. This was our first time driving in San Francisco, and we had heard the traffic was typically bad, but this seemed extreme. What would normally be a thirty-five-minute drive turned into an hour-and-a-half drive as we were trying to get from San Fran to Oakland over the Bay Bridge. By this time, the children were tired and hungry, as were we. They had numerous questions about what we would do when we arrived, when they would get to eat, and, of course, the ever popular question, "How much longer?" To say the least, my husband and I were out of patience. The kids had actually been great most of the day, but even still we were DONE and would rather have been almost anywhere else than in the car at that time.

Just as we were getting closer to our destination, we accidentally took a wrong turn and ended up getting back on the highway. We panicked and got off the highway, thinking we had solved the problem. We thought we were back on track again. This wasn't the case, however. We were actually now going back in the same direction that we had just come from. It was dark and we were all turned around, unsure which direction was the one we needed to be going in. We panicked again, and words were said that we would prefer the children not hear. My husband tried to remain calm, but it just wasn't happening. The kids must have sensed our stress, as they suddenly got very quiet. In most circumstances, I would have assured them that we would be fine and this was really not a big deal in the scheme of things. However, in this moment, I didn't have it in me. I was worried, tired, and hungry. I simply wanted to be done with this trip (yes, that quickly!).

My husband was in no mood to talk to anyone at this

point, but luckily he had a sense that what we needed more than anything at that moment was to pull over and regroup. He took the first exit that he could and pulled into a strip mall restaurant. We ordered our food and sat down to make a plan. We took out a map and looked at the navigation system on my husband's phone and explained to the kids what was happening. Because we took the time for this, we were much more successful when we began our drive again. It reminded me of the instructions we were given earlier in the day on the plane: Put your own mask on first before helping others. My husband and I were in no place to be who we needed to be until we were able to refuel and regroup ourselves. Soon enough our family found its way again.

Sometimes we need assistance in our journeys, such as asking for help, accepting a course correction, or taking time for guidance. Parenting is one of those journeys. I know many parents are looking for a guide to raising their children, even though they understand that every child is different. I've heard many parents say they've read numerous books that claim to have the solutions to their parenting struggles, but the books don't seem to help *their* child or *their* family. Many parents feel overwhelmed by the plethora of information available on raising children and are often left feeling frustrated and inadequate. Like many parents, you're probably looking for practical ways to improve your family life *and* feel a sense of control while you do this. *Your Family Compass* will provide a guide for you, yet *you* get to be in control of the process.

This book won't tell you exactly what to do in every situation with your child. However, you will gain the tools you need to make these decisions yourself after you've had the opportunity to set family goals and grow in your understanding of your child and his behaviors.

Allow me to be your guide through the five different sections: Goals, Understanding, Independence, Discussions, and Enjoyment. The areas we'll be covering will lead to creating your family compass. So when you get off track, because we all do, you have something to lead you back. My hope is that by the end of this book:

- You'll feel more confident in your parenting.

- You'll have a deeper understanding of your child and, therefore, feel closer to him.

- You'll feel equipped to help your child feel genuinely confident and successful.

- You'll be able to more fully enjoy your parenting journey.

- You'll feel as though your family has a compass to help lead you back when life throws challenges your way and you begin to feel off course.

Each section is infused with case studies from families I've worked with through the years as a teacher and parent consultant, to help the concepts come alive. All names have been changed to protect anonymity. Workbook portions provide you with a means to put the material into practice immediately.

Take time to use a visual cue as you navigate this journey called parenting. Picture the word GUIDE. You can ask yourself the following questions throughout this journey with your family:

G Am I parenting toward my family Goals?

U Do I have an Understanding of my child, and am I helping him begin to understand himself?

I Am I providing a variety of opportunities for Independence for my child?

D Do I have quality Discussions with my parenting partner and child?

E Am I Enjoying our family life more often than not?

Sometimes we forget that some of the more challenging aspects of parenting are all part of the journey. Difficulties are inevitable. However, when we have a compass for the journey, we can keep plugging along even through the hard times. When life takes us farther off course, we have something to guide us back. Now, let's get started on this adventure!

Goals

Through this first section, I'll walk you through goal-setting strategies for your family. I'll explain the importance of goals and how they've benefited families in the past and how they'll benefit your family going forward. You'll have an opportunity to set your own family goals to take with you through the rest of your journey through Your Family Compass. *As I refer to goals in this section, I'm referring to the values and characteristics you hope your children will exhibit and the type of relationship you hope to have with your children through the years.*

CHAPTER ONE
Where Are You Going?

It was a typical day in the Ryan household. Andy had already left for work, Jessica was adding the final items to the children's lunch boxes, the kids were still getting dressed, and they all needed to be out the door in less than five minutes. Jessica yelled up to the kids, "Hurry up, we have to go!" The kids came scurrying down the stairs as they were giggling and joking with each other. Jessica took one look at them and said, "Seriously, we have no time for fun! We need to get out the door. Let's go, let's go, let's go!" The kids' smiles faded, and they quickly ran to get their jackets, shoes, and backpacks to leave for school. The car ride to school was short, so luckily Jessica wasn't late for work. However, after she dropped the kids off, she felt awful. She hated that their mornings were like this every day. She wished they didn't have to be rushed and that she could actually take some time to connect with the children in the morning. In other words, Jessica wanted to actually *talk* to her kids in the morning and feel like she had time to *listen* to them.

The Ryan household is like many American households. It's easy to get so wrapped up in the day-to-day aspects of life that the big picture is forgotten. Sometimes when you take time to step back, you realize that the way you're acting or reacting to your children in certain situations may not be fostering the type of relationship you hope to have with them in the future.

How can you navigate this parenting journey if you don't know the direction you want to be heading? When you define your long-term goals and the characteristics you hope to encourage in your children, it helps create a unique plan for your family. This plan then helps you make more mindful choices for, and with, your children in a myriad of ways.

When I first started working with Andy and Jessica on the concept of long-term goals, they were stunned. They looked at each other and said, "Wow, we've done this with our finances, but it never occurred to us to do this with our parenting." When they took time to do this, they realized their goals were at odds with their current parenting practices. They both felt like they had been in survival mode with their kids. They hadn't felt like they had the time to really *think* about how things could be different.

They both felt like they had been in survival mode with their kids. They hadn't felt like they had the time to really think about how things could be different.

It was obvious to Andy and Jessica that they needed to make some changes. They wanted to improve their interactions with their children. They decided that by having more quality time with the children, they would be able to accomplish this. They decided they should start by making their mornings less rushed, so they would have time for quality interactions. After much thought and evaluation, Andy and Jessica decided they could both alter their work schedules. This meant a small pay cut for Jessica, since she decided to cut back on her hours. However, they decided it was worth it if it meant they could start their days off on a more positive note. For Andy, it meant having to get up a little earlier each day so he could come home from work earlier than he had been. This would help to provide more family time in the evenings.

With these changes, things felt better for the Ryan family. Jessica didn't feel like she needed to yell at the kids to hurry in the mornings any more. In fact, she actually had time to sit down for breakfast with them and talk about the day ahead. Even the children commented on how much better the mornings felt. Jessica felt a stronger connection with her children than she had felt in a long time. It was obvious they were meeting their goal of improving their interactions with their children. Andy and Jessica reported later that they continued to review their goals to make sure the parenting choices they were making fit with their broader family plan.

Family goals may change as your children age, so it's important to revisit them often. My husband and I review our goals when we have big family decisions to make or when we need to make a specific decision for one of our children, involving sports or school.

A few years ago, we were trying to weigh the benefits and drawbacks of sending our daughter, Maya, to kindergarten a year early. She was only going to miss the cutoff by six weeks and she was mature for her age. We agonized over the decision until we finally sat down and revisited the characteristics and values we hoped our children would have through the years:

- Respect and care for others and animals.

- Foster a strong faith.

- Develop strong problem-solving skills.

- Foster intrinsic motivation.

- Develop an appreciation of nature.

- Build self-confidence.

- Encourage independence.

Suddenly, the decision was easy. The majority of these values were included in the preschool Maya attended. Plus, since I was home with Maya many days, we would be able to spend time together hiking, biking, and gardening, which were all aspects of life we enjoyed a great deal. Ultimately, my husband and I didn't want to rush Maya out of this uniquely enriching time in her life. Thus, we decided not to send her to kindergarten early. We have not regretted this decision because we had the tools (our goals) to help us see what was best for our family and for our daughter.

Setting Goals for *Your* Family

Take the time now to consider goals for your family. This is important to do with your parenting partner. Parenting partners typically include a spouse or life partner. For some of you, it might be a grandparent, close friend, or daycare provider. Essentially, it's any other adult who helps make parenting decisions alongside you regarding your children.

I. **What *characteristics or values* do you hope your children will have as they continue to get older, move into their teen years, and then eventually reach adulthood?**

- It might be helpful to start by brainstorming a list of potential characteristics or values you admire in others. This could be done separately or together. If done separately, then compare lists and narrow them down from there.

- You can then begin to narrow your list by grouping similar characteristics together.

- There's no need to put the characteristics in order of importance, unless you prefer that method.

- See tables 1 and 2 for examples of different lists from two families.

2. What type of *relationship* do you hope to have with your children through the years, from now through adulthood?

- To start, simply think about the type of relationship you have had with your parents through the years and if this is similar to what you want with your own children or if it's different.

- Again, brainstorm a list and then narrow it down.

- See tables 1 and 2 for examples of different lists from two families.

3. **How do you want your children to describe *you* as a parent when they're adults?**

- Continue to think about the type of relationship you had with your parents growing up. Are these positive memories? If so, what aspects would you like to repeat with your own children? If not, what aspects would you like to be different?

- Do you want your children to remember you as the parent who's too busy for them and quick to get angry with them or as the parent who took time for them and was respectful of their ideas?

- This list is purely for you to think about every so often. If you find yourself parenting in a way that is not supportive of the type of parent you hope to be, it's time to regroup and make a new plan.

Examples from Two Families

Table I offers a sample list from one of the families I've spent time working with. Table IA lists the *characteristics or values* they hope their children will have as they continue to get older, move into the teen years, and then eventually reach adulthood. Table IB lists the type of *relationship* they hope to have with their children through the years.

TABLE I	
Table IA Example Family I	Table IB Example Family I
What *characteristics or values* do you hope your children will have as they continue to get older, move into the teen years, and later reach adulthood? • Internally motivated • Respect for others • Responsible • Trusting • Compassionate • Ambitious • Happy	What type of *relationship* do you hope to have with your children from now through adulthood? • Connected • Trusting • Open communication • Respectful

Table 2 is an example from another family. As you can see, every family will have its own unique list. Of course, there will be some similarities, but people want different things based on who they are, what experiences they've had, and who their children are.

TABLE 2	
Table 2A **Example Family 2**	**Table 2B** **Example Family 2**
Characteristics or values?	Relationship?
• Faith	• Caring
• A love of outdoors	• Connected
• Respect for self, others, and animals	• Choose to spend time together
• Hard working	• Supportive, but not too dependent
• Independent	
• Self-starter	
• Confident	

Building Trust

Often when I meet with families and they establish their goals, they're shocked to see how their current parenting practices aren't in line with their goals. Some of the techniques they have adopted are actually recommended in other parenting books. The problem is that there is a plethora of parenting advice given, even by experts, that doesn't take into account the long-term goals you have for your children.

There is a plethora of parenting advice given, even by experts, that doesn't take into account the long-term goals you have for your children.

17

I'd like to use the example of a family who put their child, Amal, age two, in a time out every time he lost control when he was upset. The parents, Samir and Julie, intended for this to extinguish the behavior by ignoring it. Ignoring negative behavior is not a bad technique if it's used in the right circumstances. However, Amal was not yet capable of calming himself. Amal's out-of-control behavior often got worse when his parents put him in a time out. Samir and Julie began to wonder if this was the right approach.

When we discussed Samir and Julie's long-term goals, one of the characteristics they hoped to encourage in Amal was trust in the world and in his parents. I asked them how they thought Amal felt when he was in a time out while feeling emotionally out of control. They thought he probably felt mad, scared, and even abandoned. When Julie said the last word, she teared up and said, "This is why we need a new plan. This doesn't feel right." They had this sense beforehand, but outlining their long-term goals helped clarify their feelings and give them the confidence needed to make a new plan.

You may not always be in a place emotionally to remain calm and keep your cool when your child loses control. Remember to put your own oxygen mask on first! These are times when moving away from your child briefly to take a break is essential. Of course, you need to know your child is safe before you move away from him. If you need more than a few minutes, it's time to call a friend or neighbor to help for moral support.

Samir and Julie determined that they needed to give Amal more support during these moments, even though they were stressful. If they wanted Amal to trust them and the world, they needed to show him they wouldn't abandon him, even when he was acting in undesirable ways.

Samir and Julie are just one example of how examining long-term goals for their child changed how they reacted to their child's behaviors. (I will touch on the use of time outs more in chapter five.)

Growing Connections

Paula and Chris were also surprised by the insight that goal setting brought to their perspective on their family life. Evenings and weekends felt rushed getting the kids to their sporting events. All three children played hockey from October through April. Because of this schedule, they had very little focused family time and rarely had dinners together during these months.

Neither parent liked this schedule. They knew from their own childhoods that family time was important, especially family meals where they had time to discuss their day, regroup, and simply connect. Their family used to have meals together more often when the kids were younger, before they got involved in sports. Paula and Chris had always planned on continuing to have family meals through the years, even during the busier sports season, so they felt their kids were missing out on an important bonding experience. They were fairly good about fitting meals in during the off-season, but they didn't think that was sufficient. They felt they spent most of May every year simply reconnecting and determined this wasn't the life they wanted for their family.

The couple chose to make some changes. First, they decided that they wanted to have meals together as a family four times per week. Their hope was to increase this over time. They also decided that perhaps these meals didn't have to always be dinner time. Each week, they looked ahead to their weekend and found a time on both Saturday and Sunday when they could all sit down to have a meal together. This needed to be at a time that wasn't rushed and was set aside for their family only.

During the week, they found some easy but still healthy meals that they could prepare quickly before (or sometimes after) their evening activities. They also decided to be open to having the children skip practices every once in a while if life was feeling too hectic. Their children were all still in the elementary grades, so this was more feasible than it would be if they were in high school. They explained to the coaches that family time needed to be a priority and that hockey was starting to get in the way. They discussed the need to possibly cut back. The coaches were not in complete agreement. However, Paula and Chris felt confident that being open to their children missing practice every once in a while was actually putting their family first and that was more important to them than anything else.

Making changes isn't always easy, especially when these changes may conflict with what the majority of families are choosing to do in this culture.

Making changes isn't always easy, especially when these changes may conflict with what the majority of families are choosing to do in this culture. It was obvious to Paula and Chris, as they started to implement their new goals, that they were making the right decisions for their family because they instantly felt more connected to their children, which positively influenced all areas of their family life.

When Life Takes an Unexpected Turn

I received a call from Cara explaining that she was interested in setting up a time to meet with me along with her ex-husband, Drew. She went on to tell me that two years ago Drew decided to end their marriage. The divorce was final about a year ago, but it wasn't until now that she was finally starting to feel like herself again.

Cara felt like the kids had handled the change fairly well, but she noticed that the oldest child was beginning to play one parent against the other. For example, if Cara told Claudia, age fourteen, that she had to get her homework done before going to spend time with friends, Claudia would say that her dad lets her go out before doing homework. Cara was unsure how much of this was true and how much of it was simply a ploy to get her to relax about the homework. Unfortunately, Claudia was notorious for not getting her homework done, which made it difficult for Cara to relax about this issue.

Cara realized that this behavior was common for a child Claudia's age, but she felt like the situation was more complex since she and Drew were divorced. Cara still struggled to talk with Drew at great length unless there was a third party involved. Luckily, Drew agreed that they needed to spend some time talking about their children together so Claudia wouldn't continue to play one parent against the other.

Cara, Drew, and I focused our conversation on family goals. The idea was that both parents would keep a list of these goals at their homes. Cara and Drew created these goals together during our meeting. This wasn't easy for Cara, but she was grateful that they were finding a way to align their parenting even if they weren't married any longer. Drew was also grateful, as he too was unsure how to handle those moments when Claudia would tell him Cara was allowing her to do something that he didn't think she would allow.

Setting the family goals provided Cara and Drew a compass to keep them going in the right direction in those moments of uncertainty. They agreed they needed to be better about communicating with each other so the children knew they couldn't attempt this tactic of playing one parent against the other. Having these family goals outlined helped them to gauge different situations that came up. For example, when Claudia would tell her mom that her dad lets her go out before doing homework, Cara now knew this was highly unlikely. Cara and Drew both agreed that responsibility was a characteristic they wanted to instill in their children, especially in Claudia since it didn't appear to come as naturally to her. Allowing her to go out prior to completing her homework would inadvertently teach her that getting her homework done was less important than spending time with her friends.

Cara and Drew felt like the discussion of family goals was extra important to their family since they were no longer parenting out of the same household. They needed the continuity of long-term goals to guide their day-to-day decisions now that they were making many of them on their own. They also realized that this time set aside to talk was very helpful beyond the goal setting, even though it was difficult emotionally at times. I now meet with Cara and Drew every six weeks for them to simply touch base with each other with a neutral party present. At some point, they won't need me any longer and will feel comfortable navigating this journey on their own. They'll be comfortable with their family compass. When I'm not meeting with them, their goals are their guide.

Evaluate Further

Think about your own lists of characteristics and relationships that you created earlier:

I. In what ways are your current parenting practices in line with the characteristics you hope your children will have and the type of relationship you hope you'll have with them as they continue to get older, move into the teen years, and eventually reach adulthood?

2. In what ways are your current parenting practices out of line with your family goals?

3. What changes could you make to your current parenting practices to make them more in line with your goals?

   - This is something you may choose to come back to answer after you've read further into the book.

Change Isn't Always Necessary

As you've read, there are many reasons why parents decide to make changes after outlining and reflecting on their goals. Often, parents find that their long-term goals are in sync with their current parenting practices, and defining their goals simply reaffirms what they're already doing. It's a way to check in and feel encouraged by their choices and their current family life.

Family Mission Statement

As your children approach middle childhood (ages seven and older), you can expand upon your family goals by creating a Family Mission Statement. To do this, discuss *with* your children what their hopes for your family are. Below are some topics to explore while formulating your Family Mission Statement:

- How do you want other people to describe your family?

- How many times per week do you want to have meals together?

- What are ways your family connects? How do you spend time together?

- What characteristics and values are important to your family?

Once you discuss these questions and come to an agreement everyone feels good about, you're ready to write your mission statement. It can be beneficial to post this in your house and refer back to it often. The following is an example of one family's mission statement.

Romero Family Mission Statement

Our family strives to be . . .

- Helpful to others
- Active and healthy
- Good to each other
- A connected family

We will achieve these things by . . .

- Eating family dinners together (five out of the seven days of the week)
- Going to church together
- Volunteering together and with others
- Playing together

Your Family Mission Statement

Now, take time to brainstorm with your parenting partner and/or your children (if they're old enough) how the family mission statement could look for your family.

YOUR FAMILY'S LAST NAME HERE

Family Mission Statement

Our family strives to be . . .

We will achieve these things by . . .

Why the Long-Term View?

You might be wondering why you need to think about the teen years and adulthood when your children may only be babies or toddlers right now. The reality is, what you do now will impact your children later as well as the relationship you'll have with them in the future. If you aren't caring and respectful of your children at age four, ten, and twelve, it's quite possible they won't offer *you* any respect at ages thirteen, fifteen, and beyond. It's easier to build these characteristics and relationships when your children are young than trying to do so when they're teenagers. Outlining your goals helps you to consider the long-term implications of your parenting decisions and how these impact the growth of your family.

If you aren't caring and respectful of your children at age four, ten, and twelve, it's quite possible they won't offer you any respect at ages thirteen, fifteen, and beyond.

Looking Back over the Years

Gloria and Carl now have adult children, but when their children were young they were involved in a program through their church that was focused on keeping family connections strong. The program included bimonthly family events along with one family retreat weekend each year. They spent time defining their family goals and creating a family mission statement. Most of the events were focused on living out these family goals through activities and discussions. Many times, the parents would meet on separate occasions to discuss current parenting struggles and how they should handle them based on these goals.

The other families involved were an incredible support system for Gloria and Carl through the years and continue to be good friends even now that the children are all grown. According to Gloria and Carl, the children who grew up as part of this program are all living balanced lives, are confident in who they are, and have close, interdependent relationships with their parents. The children have varied careers and family lives, but they all have grown to be well-developed people due to the strong foundation their families created.

Gloria and Carl feel that although the program was extremely helpful to them in their parenting years, it was the activity of defining their family goals that was the most impactful. They continued to revisit the goals throughout the years on decisions, such as possible job changes, allowances, college choices, possible moves, et cetera. The goals Gloria and Carl set for their family became the foundation for navigating their parenting journey.

Your Family Compass

You've now had a chance to set family goals for your family, hear how goal setting has been beneficial for other families, and think about the idea of a Family Mission Statement. This is an essential step in creating a compass for your family. Now, let's move on to Understanding, the second fundamental step in this process.

Understanding

Throughout this section of the book, you'll learn how to determine where your child is developmentally, why she behaves the way she does, and how to approach common parenting struggles.

- *Chapter two is a very important walk through research-based best practices in child psychology. This is well worth the read to gain a better understanding of how children take in the world around them.*

- *In chapter three, you'll explore the reasons behind children's puzzling behaviors and ways to react to those behaviors.*

- *In chapter four, you'll examine some of the more challenging temperament traits your child might be exhibiting. This will help you gain a deeper appreciation of her and how to begin to help her learn to manage these traits.*

- *Chapter five focuses on the fact that raising children is a process. Everyone makes mistakes as they learn. You and your child are not immune to this.*

With time and attention given to this task throughout this journey, you'll have a well-working compass to help guide you. As you build upon your knowledge, you'll not only begin to understand your child better, but also yourself and your parenting style. This increased awareness will help you connect more fully with your child during each stage of development.

CHAPTER TWO
All You Really Need to Know from Child Psychology 101

Recently, I received a distressed call from Kendra regarding her two-year-old son Max. She told me that she felt her discipline method wasn't working, but she didn't know what else to try. She said that Max was constantly getting into things around the house. He didn't seem to understand the word "no" and had a difficult time focusing on activities for longer than a few minutes. It was apparent that Kendra felt overwhelmed by Max's behavior. However, I sensed her feelings were intensified by the worry that something might be wrong with Max because of his active nature and short attention span.

Kendra's concerns are common. Many parents worry if their child is exhibiting abnormal behaviors. The trouble is, such worries often create more stress on families than is warranted. Once you know what's in the realm of normal development, you can more confidently decide whether or not to seek help for your child when difficulties arise. This knowledge also helps you set realistic expectations for your child.

> *Once you know what's in the realm of normal development, you can more confidently decide whether or not to seek help for your child when difficulties arise.*

Although some of you may find it interesting to delve more deeply into the study of child psychology, I'll simply be covering the essentials needed for your parenting journey. This will be a useful tool to continue to come back to through the years as your child ages and as your family grows.

Erikson's Developmental Stages

Erik Erikson (1902–1994), an American developmental psychologist and psychoanalyst, is well known for his theory of social development. Although this is termed a *social theory*, it's very much a theory on *emotional development* as well.

Erik Erikson's Theory on Developmental Stages

Infant (0–1 yrs): *Trust vs. Mistrust*

Toddler (1–3 yrs): *Autonomy vs. Shame and Doubt*

Preschooler (3–6 yrs): *Initiative vs. Guilt*

School Age (6–11 yrs): *Industry vs. Inferiority*

Adolescent (12–18 yrs): *Identity vs. Role Confusion*

Young Adult (19–30 yrs): *Intimacy vs. Isolation*

Middle-Age Adult (30+): *Generativity vs. Stagnation*

As you can see, after each developmental level there are two emotional responses presented as though they are combating one another. The first is the desired emotional response that is sought out for children from infancy through middle age. Erikson believed that the favorable response in each stage of development needed to be attained for people to move successfully into the next stage of development. If, instead, the second emotional response was achieved, the child wouldn't move successfully into the following stage, therefore setting the child up for later struggles.

Infancy (0–1 Years): Seeking Trust

During the *Infancy Stage*, it's crucial to create an environment that encourages the child to trust the world around him, his caregivers, and himself. This is why it's best for parents to answer babies' cries until the parents have a better sense of what each cry means. When your infant cries for you because she needs something physically or emotionally, it's important to respond to those cries. There are many times, however, children cry because they're upset and aren't in need of anything beyond some words of comfort and encouragement. It takes time to learn the difference between these various cries.

When an infant is fed when she's hungry and is warmed when she's cold, she learns that the world is a trustworthy place. Gradually, you can teach your child how to begin to trust *herself* by helping her learn how to comfort herself. You might offer your baby a special blanket or teddy bear to hug when you move into another room to grab the laundry, for example. You can offer words of encouragement and love as you teach this skill. You can say, "I know you're sad. You have your blanket. I'm right over here." Then as soon as you can get back to the infant, remain calm and say, "Now that wasn't so bad, was it? Even though I couldn't hold you, I was close by." This reaffirms the baby's trust in you and the world, and it begins to form a trust in herself.

When an infant is fed when she's hungry and is warmed when she's cold, she learns that the world is a trustworthy place.

A strong parent-child attachment is essential for positive social and emotional development. Developmental psychologist Dr. Marti Erickson states, "Children who have a secure attachment at one year old are more likely at later ages to be confident, cooperative, caring, and able to manage their emotions and impulses in an acceptable way." Dr. Erickson has conducted research at the University of Minnesota for many years and has dedicated her career to linking research on attachment to practice and public policy. She agrees that although a secure parent-child attachment doesn't prevent all issues, it certainly creates some resiliency and a foundation for further relationships.

Tips for this stage:

- Answer an infant's cries as soon as you can until you can decipher between the different cries. Once you can decipher between cries, you can determine how quickly you need to attend to the baby.

- Offer the infant comfort through physical touch and words.

- Gradually teach the infant how to begin to trust and comfort herself.

Toddler (1–3 Years): Seeking Autonomy

During the *Toddler Stage*, it's essential to provide an environment where the child can explore fully. The child needs to begin to feel a sense of autonomy in the space that he's in. The toddler-aged child needs choices within limits. When you child-proof your home, your child can have a sense of autonomy, but also he has an understanding of his limits. You, of course, still need to supervise your child, but it eliminates the need for the child to be followed around every inch of the house. Children, during the toddler years, tend to hear the word "no" a great deal. This becomes discouraging, and some children feel defeated by this and take on feelings of shame and doubt. Your child needs to know that you understand that he has his own thoughts and ideas.

The toddler-aged child needs choices within limits.

You've likely experienced how frustrating it is to take your toddler-aged child somewhere that isn't childproofed. It seems as though the child is constantly getting into things during these times. This can begin to feel like defiance when in reality it's simply that children this age NEED to explore and gain a sense of control. When children are able to explore and have control of some aspects of their life (toileting, deciding between two choices for breakfast, etc.), they feel a sense of autonomy that's crucial to this age. It's important to note that when adults over-emphasize the idea of a child being a "big kid," the child might begin to feel ambivalence about his autonomy. He might wonder if he wants to even get bigger. There's no need to get overly excited about his independence, but rather approach it with a matter-of-fact tone: "Let me show you how you can carry your plate to the counter. I can tell your arms are strong enough to do this . . . Thanks for your help." This leads to successfully moving onto the next stage, feeling confident and secure. I will touch more on autonomy and independence in chapter six.

Tips for this stage:

- Childproof your home and the other environments your child spends time in.

- Allow time and space for your child to explore and be active.

- Provide your child with choices: "Will you wear the blue shirt or the red shirt today?"

- Allow your child to have some independence. A few examples of that include letting him do the following:

  - Carry his plate to the counter after a meal.

- Get a cereal box out of the cabinet.

- Begin to pour water or milk out of a small pitcher.

- Walk beside the stroller instead of sitting in it.

- Climb into his car seat on his own.

- Learn to use the toilet with guidance.

- Refer to appendix I for more examples.

Preschooler (3–6 Years): Seeking Initiative

During the *Preschooler Stage*, the objective is to encourage the child's initiative. Preschool-age children are constantly making plans, sharing ideas, and attempting to do more on their own. This can be hard when *you* have a plan and a schedule. When your child is taking on more responsibilities of his own (which can actually begin in the toddler years), you, as his parent, need to make more time in your day for this. You'll now need ten minutes to get shoes and jackets on, whereas before, when you put the shoes and jacket on *for* your child, you only needed five. This is well worth the extra time as it will lead to your child feeling confident in his abilities and ideas.

Preschool-age children are constantly making plans, sharing ideas, and attempting to do more on their own.

It's important to help your child know he's being heard and that he's respected. However, it's sometimes challenging to find a balance between the child having some control and the child having more control than he's developmentally ready for. I'll delve into this more deeply in chapter six.

Tips for this stage:

- Acknowledge the child's thoughts and ideas.

- Be sure the child has numerous opportunities to be independent. A few examples are allowing her to do the following:

  - Begin to help with food preparation.

  - Feed pets with supervision.

  - Help sort laundry.

  - Refer to appendix 1 for more examples.

- Begin using family discussions as a tool for making changes within your family. I will discuss this further in chapter nine.

I've found many phrases to be helpful over the years when working with preschool-aged children. For example, as your young child runs back into the house after you've just come out together, the simple phrase of "What's your plan?" will provide you with a window into what he's aiming to accomplish in that moment. This phrase is positive, rather than punitive, which will set your child at ease so he can be honest with you about his plans. He knows you're interested in his ideas too. Appendix 2 provides more examples of helpful phrases. These words are especially helpful as the preschool child is seeking initiative, but they can be used with younger and older children as well.

School Age (6–11 Years): Seeking Industry

During the *School Age Stage*, children are beginning to sort out who they are. Children during this stage judge themselves based on what they're capable of doing. A child quickly can see if she's not measuring up to the other children she spends time with. It's imperative for teachers, parents, and coaches to eliminate comparisons of children based on their abilities. There's no need to point these things out, as many children are already aware of their abilities in comparison to others. Having an adult point them out creates feelings of inferiority.

During the School Age Stage, children are beginning to sort out who they are.

A child may still begin to have a sense of inferiority even without the "help" of adults. You can assist these children by talking with them about the fact that everyone has strengths and weaknesses or growth areas. It's beneficial to expose your child to a variety of activities, so she has an opportunity to see what her options might be and where she might find the most success. This doesn't mean to pack your child's schedule full of activities. Instead, gradually over time, try a variety of things. Many of the activities that you could choose to sign your child up for through an organization could also be done for free in your own backyard or house and done together as a family. For example, if your child thinks she enjoys running, you don't need to sign her up for a running team right away; you could simply decide that you and she will run together a couple times a week to try it out.

Tips for this stage:

- Allow your child to try a variety of experiences, so she can begin to see what might be her "thing."

- Be mindful of overscheduling your child, as children this age still need time to simply play. Oftentimes, the variety mentioned above can be found in your own backyard.

- Talk as a family about the fact that everyone has different strengths and weaknesses.

- Aim to have high but realistic expectations for your child; don't insist on perfection, as it sets a child up for failure.

- Let your child see that you make mistakes too and how you can bounce back from these moments.

- Take extreme caution when considering the use of comparisons between children. If it won't be sending a positive message to the children involved, then it shouldn't be said for them to hear.

Adolescence (12–18 Years): Seeking Identity

During the *Adolescence Stage*, the child is beginning to integrate many roles into his life. He begins to take more ownership for the relationships he has. He realizes he's a brother, son, friend, athlete, and student, but he is still learning how to integrate all of these roles into his life. There are more social expectations. For example, if the child doesn't spend some time focusing on his friends and only spends time with his family, he'll likely begin to lose those friends. If he puts all his emphasis on his sports, he may struggle to keep up with the role he has of being a student.

You'll continue to guide your child during this stage; however, this is the time where you'll begin to gradually let go of your control of his scheduling and studies. You'll remain connected, spending time together and continuing that close relationship. However, you need to provide your child with independence during this time. If you're afraid your child might fail in certain situations, you sometimes have to allow that to happen. He needs to see that his parents will not always be there to rescue him. You'll always love him, but you can't always rescue. For example, if your child's struggling to get his homework done after football practice each night, it's your job to inform him that until he gets his homework turned in on time, he won't be able to attend football practices or games. School must come first. In chapter six, I'll discuss further how to present this to the child beforehand. Some parents feel they should stay up late to complete the child's homework for him, call the teacher to get an extension on his homework, or stay up later with him while he finishes his homework. However, this will be doing a disservice to the child in the long run as he won't be taking this on as his own responsibility.

You'll continue to guide your child during this stage; however, this is the time where you'll begin to gradually let go of your control of his scheduling and studies.

Children during this stage also begin to form ideas about their identity based on who they spend time with. This can be a great thing if your child is choosing friends who work hard at school and have close family connections. However, this doesn't always happen. You can gain insight into how your child views himself by the friends he chooses. If your child is consistently choosing friends who are lacking confidence, you need to begin to look at what you can do to help your child build his confidence. If you outright tell your teen he can't remain friends with a certain group of friends, it will likely cause him to pull away from his relationship with you. However, you can focus on building your own child's self-confidence by seeking out an activity that he might really enjoy on his own or with you. Perhaps he could take part in a sport he hasn't tried or a weekend job helping a neighbor with yard work. The idea would be that the child would gradually have more faith in himself and eventually decide on his own that he might want different friends.

The adolescent who's not allowed to make some decisions on his own and feels like his parents are always trying to make their ideas and opinions his won't be able to successfully move beyond this stage of development. He not only will feel resentment, but he also won't have the opportunity to form his own identity. Oftentimes when teens feel oppressed by their parents, they choose something completely opposite to believe in or do, simply out of rebellion. The child is left feeling even more confused about who he is and who he wants to be.

Tips for this stage:

- Continue to keep a close, connected relationship with your child during this stage, but step back a bit so your adolescent can begin to form his own identity and beliefs about the world.

- Don't rescue your child. Everyone, even children and teenagers, need to fall down sometimes. If they don't fall down they won't know how to get themselves back up again.

- Be aware of who your teen's friends are. Get to know these friends, so you know how your child likely views himself.

- Encourage your teen to reflect on the relationships he has. Encourage him to think about what his friends bring out in him, for better or for worse.

- For further reading on adolescent development, I recommend psychologist Dr. David Walsh's 2004 book, *Why Do They Act That Way? A Survival Guide to the Adolescent Brain for You and Your Teen.*

Young Adult (Roughly 19–30 Years): Seeking Intimacy

In the *Young Adult Stage*, many adults are beginning to commit themselves to another person and eventually some of these adults become parents. You likely know adults who didn't successfully pass through the previous stage of development, as they continuously seem to struggle to incorporate the many roles they hold in their lives. It's very challenging to be a spouse, parent, and professional all at the same time. Imagine how much harder this would be if you never really had the opportunity to learn who you truly are.

During this stage, your child will continue to change and grow as a person and get to know herself even better with time. Her world will broaden as she seeks intimacy with others beyond family, even more so than she did in the teen years. Her desire and need to have deep, intimate relationships with others (friends, partners, or spouses) will increase and solidify. Your relationship with your young adult child can still be very close, and for some, it's even closer than it ever has been; however, it's beneficial for her to have intimate relationships beyond her family of origin.

Tips for this stage:

- Continue to be available as an emotional support as needed for your young adult child; however, refrain from rescuing.

- Let her know you have confidence in her choices.

- However, if you have concerns with her intimate relationships, share these with her in a nonjudgmental and supportive way.

Middle-Age (Roughly 30-Plus): Seeking Generativity or Productivity

I am moving briefly from information about your child to discussing *you* in the *Middle-Age Stage* of Erikson's developmental theory. Erikson's stages continue on beyond this stage, but for the purposes of this book, I'm only including these first seven. It's important, as a parent, to assess where you are developmentally as well. This provides a guide to base some of your parenting decisions on.

During the *Middle-Age Stage*, adults seek satisfaction through productivity—whether it be in raising a family, working in a professional career, or through volunteering. Productivity (generativity) is very important for you to keep in mind throughout your parenting journey. If you feel stagnant rather than generative, it will be very challenging for you to be the parent you hope to be. You might begin to feel resentment or frustration toward your children since oftentimes they might be the

Productivity (generativity) is very important for you to keep in mind throughout your parenting journey.

roadblock to fulfilling your productive needs since parenting takes so much time.

If you've chosen to stay home with your children, you may have given up, or put on hold, a professional career. This can be a wonderful decision for a family, but you need to be mindful of how you'll be able to fulfill yourself in this generative way. I've known numerous stay-at-home parents (moms and dads) who *did* feel as though they were contributing to their society in a productive way while they were home. Different things fulfill different people emotionally. In other words, what is fulfilling to one, may not be fulfilling to another.

Whether you're staying at home with your children or working part or full time, it's incredibly important, as a parent, to step back every so often and assess this situation. Do you feel productive? If not, how could you begin to feel this way? I have known some parents, after thinking about this, who've chosen to start working again. Rachel, a mom I worked with a couple of years ago, was one of these parents who decided to go back to work after being home for a year with her three young children. She unfortunately felt guilty about this decision, but she later realized that she was actually a better parent because of this. Rachel was feeling too stagnant at home, and this was preventing her from being the parent she wanted to be. Once she felt a sense of generativity again, she began parenting the way she knew she was capable of.

I've also worked with parents who decided to take on volunteer projects when they have felt stagnant. It provided them with the mental stimulation that they felt they were lacking. This helped them be better parents because they were more satisfied with their contributions to the world around them. I've also worked with parents who were employed outside of the home and felt they were missing out on the simple pleasures they wished they could share with their children. Some of these parents sought ways to strike a better balance, knowing their careers would be waiting for them as their children got older. I've also worked with many parents who decided to leave their jobs to be home with their children, even though prior to having children they were certain they would continue working outside of the home. To them, they knew they would feel the most generative being with their children full time. These decisions are difficult to make and are very personal. Erikson's developmental stages provide you with a framework to understand why you might feel the way you do. When you understand your feelings and have the ability to examine your family goals, these decisions don't seem quite so daunting.

How Are Erikson's Stages of Development Affected by Adoption?

If your child is adopted, Erikson's developmental stages may need to be shifted. For example, if you're adopting a child who is three, you might need to assume she's in the infant stage of development and that she'll need to learn to trust you and perhaps the world around her. As you're getting to know your newly adopted child, you'll want to be sure to answer her

So although she may have gone through these stages with her previous caregiver, she'll need to go through this with you as her new parent.

cries until you can decipher between them, even if your child is three years old or ten years old. She's trying to figure out if she can trust you. So although she may have gone through these stages with her previous caregiver, she'll need to go through this with you as her new parent. The time frame she spends in these stages will depend a great deal on the circumstances she was in prior to the adoption, her level of care, and the quality of her attachment to others.

Erikson's Developmental Stages & Your Child

Erikson's developmental stages certainly don't tell you all about development, but most of the time they provide enough of a framework to remind you of where your child is developmentally. You can use this as a mental check-in. For example, you can think to yourself each day, "Did I provide ways for my toddler to feel autonomy today? If not, how could I incorporate more of this tomorrow?" or "Am I stepping back enough from my adolescent child's world to allow her to explore and take ownership for her many roles?" Your child needs your guidance to successfully navigate these stages.

Evaluate Further

If you're interested in contemplating this more as it pertains to your own child, take time to think about the questions below. This will help increase your awareness of how these stages look and how you can begin to put this information into action at home.

1. Thinking about the above information, which stage is my child currently in?

2. What are some signs that my child is in this stage? In other words, what is he doing or saying that helps me know this is the current stage?

3. What am I currently doing that is supporting this stage of development?

4. What are things I could improve to support this stage more fully for my child?

Vygotsky's Social Development Theory

I often get questions from parents about when their child will be able to do certain tasks. It's very dependent on many different aspects. Every child is different. Even though there might be a general age that most children are capable of doing certain tasks or understanding certain subject matters, not all children will acquire these abilities at the same time. Children have a variety of interactions with different people in their lives. A child's ability to understand a concept or task will depend heavily on who the child spends time with—whether it's peers his own age, children older than him, or adults.

Lev Vygotsky coined the term zone of proximal development (ZPD), which is the point from where a child is capable of performing a task or understanding a situation *with* the help of an older child, peer, or adult. Figure I shows the ZPD steps.

Figure I: Zone of Proximal Development (ZPD)

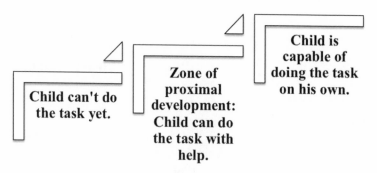

Toilet training can be an example of what the ZPD looks like. Jake began to notice that his son, Henry, would move into the other room when he needed to go to the bathroom in his diaper. Jake understood this meant that Henry was capable of knowing when his body needed to eliminate. Jake began to have Henry sit on the toilet every couple of hours to show him that instead of leaving the room to go to the bathroom in his diaper, he could go in the toilet. At this point, Henry was capable of learning to use the bathroom, but he was not yet capable of using the bathroom on his own without reminders (see figure 2). Most children won't begin to use the toilet on their own and many won't seem excited about the process either way. However, by Jake catching Henry when he was showing signs of readiness, Jake was able to build upon (also called scaffolding) this ZPD. In other words, Jake had noticed what Henry's body knew and then built upon it, so one day Henry will be able to use the toilet on his own.

Figure 2: ZPD Representing Toilet Training Example

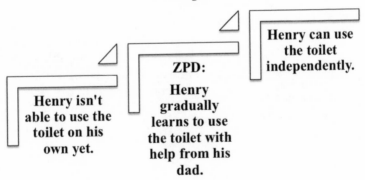

Henry isn't able to use the toilet on his own yet.

ZPD:

Henry gradually learns to use the toilet with help from his dad.

Henry can use the toilet independently.

While assessing when a child is ready for something or will be able to do something, it's important to look at two things:

1. What the child currently knows
2. Who the child spends time with

In other words, will the adults who spend time with your child be able to observe these moments of readiness to expand on what the child knows and what the child is capable of learning?

I think of this in relation to children learning how to be a part of a group. For some children, this comes naturally. They enjoy coming together with their class to hear the plan for the day or to listen to a story or sing. Others need help and guidance during these times to learn what's expected of them. When a three-year-old child starts preschool, she may not yet be capable of sitting with the group for more than a few minutes. However, a teacher can sit with her during this time to help stretch her a little further, so she will gradually be able to do this on her own.

Another aspect of Vygotsky's social development theory is the idea that it's most natural for children to learn new skills and refine old skills when activities and learning are hands-on. This means children should experience more child-led learning as opposed to adult-led learning. With child-led learning, there should be a caring adult available to build upon what the children know and are learning

> *It's most natural for children to learn new skills and refine old skills when activities and learning are hands-on.*

and to offer words of encouragement. For example, your child will be better equipped with math skills if she has the opportunity to experiment with math toys and work on a variety of real-life math problems, such as measuring how long a table is in relation to where it might be placed in the classroom, rather than listening to an adult talk about math or watching an adult do math. Likewise, your child is more likely to learn more about a sheep by petting and caring for a sheep than if she simply reads about a sheep in a book.

When choosing schools and creating activities for your children and family, you want to keep Vygotsky's social development theory in mind. When a child isn't feeling successful in school, perhaps he's struggling to sit still or is disruptive during the day; you need to assess what else might be going on. You'll want to look to see if the learning is developmentally appropriate. In other words, is it hands-on? Does he feel engaged in the learning? If not, is it too challenging for the child? Does he need assistance to pull him closer to the ZPD? Is the work too easy for him? If so, what could be done to add that extra challenge? Vygotsky's theory can help create a framework for you to understand what type of programming and education you should expect for your children.

Evaluate Further

To begin to put Vygotsky's social development theory into practice as it pertains to your child, take time to think about the following questions:

I. **What new skills is my child currently trying to develop?**

2. What existing skills is my child trying to refine?

3. How do I know when my child is ready to take on a new task:

    *   With help?

    *   By himself?

4. How can I scaffold this task to ease in the transition?

5. What other adults need to be on board with this?

Maslow's Hierarchy of Needs

In 1943, Abraham Maslow developed a theory of psychology based on human growth. Maslow's belief was that all humans have needs, and these need to be focused on in a specific order: from the bottom of a pyramid up. If your most basic needs (food, shelter, sleep, etc.) aren't met, you won't be able to put any focus on the higher level needs. This is true for all people, but especially children. The tricky part is that children aren't always able to communicate their needs to us.

Figure 3: Maslow's Hierarchy of Needs

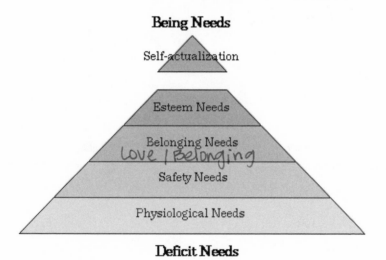

Developed by Dr. C. George Boeree (2006), former professor of psychology at Shippensburg University in Pennsylvania from Abraham Maslow's original Hierarchy of Needs Pyramid

Figure 3 shows the different needs in the order of importance. As discussed, a child who isn't getting his most basic needs met won't be able to attach to his caregivers and will certainly not be able to focus and understand limits. Likewise, if the child is in an unsafe situation at school or at home, he will struggle to make friends and connect with his teacher unless serious intervention takes place.

One extremely important but often overlooked aspect of Maslow's Hierarchy of Needs is the role of perception. Not only does it matter if a child *is* getting his basic needs met or *is* safe, it's important that the child *perceives* the situation as such. For example, you might know your child is in a safe situation at school, but if he doesn't *feel* safe he'll struggle to connect with his class-

Not only does it matter if a child is getting his basic needs met or is safe, it's important that the child perceives the situation as such.

mates and teachers. This is true for children who don't *feel* connected to or liked by their teachers. They will not be able to achieve at the level they're capable of if a solid student–teacher connection is lacking.

Be mindful of Maslow's Hierarchy of Needs when examining issues you encounter with your children. First, you need to look at the bottom layers to make sure your child has his basic needs met. You have likely experienced moments where your child is melting down because he's hungry or tired. In these moments, since the child's most basic needs aren't met, he won't be able to behave in the way that you know he typically would. This shouldn't be used as an excuse for the child's negative behavior; however, this helps to understand the behavior better.

Once you've been in this situation, you become more prepared by making sure your child has food when he'll need it and that he's getting adequate sleep, for example.

Once you know your child's basic needs have been met and you know he *feels* safe, you can begin to look at how he's perceiving the relationships that he has. Some children, because of their temperament, are more susceptible to feelings of insecurity. You need to be aware of this sensitivity and acknowledge that you may need to spend more time connecting with this child than another child who is less sensitive. I will discuss this more in chapter four.

Evaluate Further

To begin to put Maslow's Hierarchy of Needs into practice as it pertains to your family life, take time to consider the following questions:

I.   What's an example of a situation I've observed where I knew my child was safe, but he didn't feel safe?

2.   When have I noticed that my child was stuck at a particular level?

3. How can I help to address these challenges or perceived challenges?

4. What other adults could get on board to help fill the need and advance my child upward?

Did All of This Information Help Kendra with Max?

At the beginning of this chapter, we met Kendra and her two-year-old son, Max. When Kendra and I discussed the concerns she had about her son, she was quickly put at ease to hear that Max was very much in the realm of normal development. Instead of viewing his active, curious behavior as defiance, she began viewing it as exploration and learning. She was excited to see all that he was observing and was able to expand on those observations by teaching him new things. Max actually began to talk more than he had been previously because he and Kendra were engaging in conversations more.

Kendra also realized that even though Max appeared to be unfocused at times, it didn't mean she couldn't help him gain more focus in some situations. When Max didn't want to sit at the dinner table when he ate, she now knew that he was capable of learning how to do this since he could do this with help. She noticed this opportunity as the ZPD. Kendra also realized that when Max seemed the most resistent to redirection was when he was very tired. She began to keep track of when this was happening, so she could put him down for a nap before he got overtired. Kendra had been viewing his resistance as defiance, but once she realized it was because his most basic needs were not being met (i.e., Maslow's Hierarchy of Needs), she had a greater understanding of why he was acting the way he was. Overall, Kendra was relieved to know that her son was okay and that his behaviors now made more sense. The following summarizes this in terms of the theories.

Summary: Use of Theories

Kendra was reassured by Erikson's stages of development.

She was able to recognize ZPDs and take advantage of that.

She could identify her son's place on Maslow's pyramid and his need to advance upward.

Gaining a better understanding of basic child psychology can help you understand your child better and offer reassurance when you're unsure of what is expected at each age. When you grasp how children learn best and are able to determine when learning is optimal, it provides a framework for examining the way you spend time with your child and the types of programming you involve your child in. As an added bonus, it also helps you understand yourself better. You can see how you may or may not have moved through Erikson's stages of development over the years and where you fall on Maslow's Hierarchy of Needs to help you be the parent you need to be for your child.

CHAPTER THREE
Making Sense of
Children's Behaviors

I received a call from a frustrated mom, Asia, last fall regarding her ten-year-old son, Javan. At home he was quick to argue with any request his parents had of him and usually put off doing his regular chores until his parents stood right next to him as he did them. Asia was frustrated with this for many reasons, but mainly because she didn't have time to give him reminders constantly and sit with him during his chores. Besides Javan, Asia and her husband had three other children, ages one, three, and four. At school Javan often interrupted his teachers by making jokes during class. His teachers were starting to be concerned about this behavior. Asia tried numerous techniques, such as taking away privileges, rewarding him for positive behavior, and punishing him by sending him to his room. However, none of them seemed to work. These techniques are commonly recommended when children "misbehave," but they don't get to the root of the problem.

There are various reasons why children behave negatively. You need to react differently based on the reason for the behavior. In this chapter, I'll be going over ten common reasons why children exhibit adverse behaviors. I use these ten when working with families to determine the root of the negative behaviors so I can make a plan of action for the family with the parents. I've also used these with my own children and with the children I work with when I'm teaching. Most of the time children aren't trying to be "bad"; rather, they have mistaken goals or mistaken behaviors. In other words, Javan's behavior was likely stemming from something beyond the situation. It's important to seek out what that something is and approach the issue accordingly.

Rudolph Dreikurs

Attention getting, power seeking, revenge seeking, and displaying inadequacy are the four categories of mistaken goals pursued by children, which social psychologist Rudolph Dreikurs outlines in his 1964 book, *Children: The Challenge*. Determining which of these mistaken goals your child is pursuing is the first step in deciding how to proceed or react to his behavior.

> **Goals for Mistaken Behavior, Dreikurs, 1964**
>
> *Attention Getting*
>
> *Power Seeking*
>
> *Revenge Seeking*
>
> *Displaying Inadequacy*

Attention-Getting Behavior

Attention-getting behavior is any behavior that's being done to get the attention of another person. For example, a child who hits his brother as he looks at his mom and dad is likely lashing out at his brother to get his parents' attention. Another example is the child who continues to get out of his bed asking for a drink of water or food or "one last hug."

When your child exhibits attention-getting behaviors, it's important to avoid giving him attention during this time. So, when he hits his brother while looking at you, go to the injured child, rather than the one who hit. Although it's important for the child who just hit to know his behavior isn't okay, this isn't the time to teach this since his goal is attention seeking. In other words, he isn't really trying to hurt his brother in that moment, but he is trying to get your attention. If you address this with a long discussion at the time, his goal has been achieved and he will continue to try to gain attention in this way at other times.

When your child exhibits attention-getting behaviors, it's important to avoid giving him attention during this time.

The child who continues to get out of bed trying to seek your attention should either be ignored completely, if the child is old enough for this to be safe, or you can simply pick him up and put him back into bed without any words. Even though you may be feeling angry at this time, it's beneficial to do this without showing this anger to your child.

When your child is seeking attention, it doesn't matter to him if he gains positive or negative attention as long as he gets some response. Although it's important for you to know how to handle different situations with your child, it's equally helpful to know what you can do to help prevent some of these situations in the future.

Ask Yourself the Following Questions:

- Is he getting a sufficient amount of attention at other times during the day?

- Is this the only way he gets my full attention lately?

- Do my child and I have a strong parent–child connection right now? In other words, does he feel connected to me and do I feel connected to him?

What Can You Do?

- If it's found that your child hasn't been getting much attention from you lately, set aside some one-on-one time with him.

- If the attention-getting behavior is prevalent at certain times of day, make a plan for how that time of day could go better by preparing him ahead of time with something to do.

Many parents I know have set aside a special bin of toys or projects for their children to partake in when mom or dad needs to make some phone calls or feed the baby. Other parents I've worked with tend to struggle during dinner preparation. To overcome this struggle, you can either involve your child in the cooking process or set up an activity right before the preparation time that your child can do independently. If he's older, you can have a candid conversation with him so he understands that you need to focus on getting dinner ready. Then ask him if there is anything he will need *before* you get started cooking.

Power-Seeking Behavior

Power-seeking behavior is any behavior that aims to result in gaining power over the parent. An example is the child who, when told it's time to leave the park, says she's not leaving or runs away from the parent. Power-seeking behavior often involves a child who's quick to argue or say "no" to the parent.

Power-seeking behavior is very common, especially among children two to four years old. Children these ages often feel as though they don't have any control over their lives. The amount of control a child will be allowed to have will depend on the child's age. However, all children—and adults, for that matter—have a genuine and inborn need to feel powerful. Oftentimes, these control issues get worse if they haven't successfully been addressed in the younger years.

Most of the time when a child is exhibiting power-seeking behavior it means she's lacking control in her life, or at least perceives this to be true.

Most of the time when a child is exhibiting power-seeking

behavior it means she's lacking control in her life, or at least perceives this to be true. There are many ways to boost a child's sense of control. Oftentimes, the recommendations seem completely separate from what the issue is; however, these recommendations tend to go a long way in eliminating most of the power-seeking behaviors.

Ask Yourself the Following Questions:

- Does my child have a sense of control over any aspects of her life?

- If so, what aspects? Is this enough or not enough for this age?

What Can You Do?

- Start examining your child's day from the minute she wakes. She should be able to have some control over what she wears each day. If she's wearing a uniform to school, then perhaps she can have control over the socks she wears or the undershirt she puts on.

- At breakfast time, your child should be able to choose between a couple different options to eat and take responsibility for getting this breakfast on her own (within reason, of course, depending on your child's age).

- Your child can help clear her dishes and load the dishwasher and can even help pack her own lunch with guidance.

- At bedtime she can decide what book will be read or what song to sing.

- See appendix 1 for more ideas.

When a child feels more in control of her surroundings, she's less likely to lash out and question the power that you have as her parent. I will share more information regarding control and power in chapter six.

In the moment that a child is exhibiting power-seeking behavior, the parent can show empathy for her desire to want control. However, it's important to not give in to this behavior because doing so will only encourage this type of behavior in the future. Use simple phrases such as, "You wish you could go play with your friend, but that's not an option now. Let's think about when you could do that a different time." Refer to appendix 2 for more examples.

Revenge-Seeking Behavior

Revenge-seeking behavior is any behavior that's aimed to hurt the parent, either emotionally or physically. At this point, the child feels helpless. When the child has tried to get her parents' attention or tried to gain power and has not succeeded at either, she will likely move to revenge-seeking behaviors. When a child hits, pushes, or starts yelling at or cursing at her parents, she's trying to get revenge. Usually a child has started with a different subconscious goal and moved to this point.

The reality is once your child is in revenge-seeking mode, she loses her ability to really hear what you're saying when trying to address the issue.

When your child pursues revenge-seeking behavior, it's important for you to step back and reassess what's going wrong.

What did this start as: attention getting or power seeking? Likely, it will have started from one of these, and you must address the situation accordingly. The reality is once your child is in revenge-seeking mode, she loses her ability to really hear what you're saying when trying to address the issue. It will take time for your child to calm down and be at a place where she can hear you again. I will discuss this more in chapter four.

When faced with revenge-seeking behaviors, you need to avoid giving in to the behavior. Your child shouldn't be allowed to hit or push you. You may need to move to a location where she can't get to you until she calms down or you may need to hold her so she can't hurt herself or anyone else. These are not easy situations. Remaining calm will help maintain the positive relationship you hope to have with your child. If your child speaks disrespectfully to you, keep in mind that your child most likely doesn't mean what she's saying in the moment. You can reflect the child's feelings back to her by saying, "You are so angry!" She probably feels like no one is on her side. Although disrespectful words should not be tolerated, the bigger issue is that these moments are signs that it's time to make a new plan so things can go differently in the future.

Ask Yourself the Following Questions:

- Are these revenge-seeking behaviors beginning as attention-getting behavior or power-seeking behavior?
- Why might my child feel like no one is on her side?

What Can You Do?

- Work to help your child know that you are on her side.

- Reflect your child's feelings back to her: "You must be so angry!"

- Ask the child, "What can we do to help you feel less angry?"

- Evaluate the reactions your child typically gets from you, her siblings, and her teachers.

- Help her see herself in a positive light.

If your child quickly moves to revenge-seeking behavior, it might be time to seek out some assistance from a professional ✓ to help assess how she can begin to feel differently about her interactions and behaviors.

Displaying Inadequacy

When a child continuously says he can't do something, he's often showing signs that he's feeling inadequate. When a child says he can't tie his shoes or put on his pants when he's capable, he might be trying to gain your attention. Or, he might be trying to tell you that he really thinks he can't do those things. Oftentimes, when a parent sees her child struggling with a zipper or shoe, especially when the family is trying to get out the door, the

The parent means well; however, the message sent to the child is that he can't do it and that he really does need mom to help him.

71

parent jumps in to rescue the child. The parent zips the coat for the child or puts the shoe on for him. The parent means well; however, the message sent to the child is that he can't do it and that he really does need mom to help him.

When a child more than three years old is continuously saying he can't do something, it's time to assess why this is happening. Perhaps the child is truly not capable of doing the activity on his own yet. If this is the case, the parent can do the activity with the child until he's capable of doing it on his own (think back to Vygotsky's zone of proximal development). For example, socks can be tricky for a three-year-old to put on by himself. However, if the parent gets the sock scrunched up so it's on the child's toes, the child can pull the sock up on his own beyond that point. The child is left feeling proud that he did it. The parent will gradually begin to allow the child to try pulling it over his toes on his own. A helpful phrase for moments when children feel they can't do something on their own is "I can help you by teaching you how." These are empowering words for everyone to hear, especially for a child.

Ask Yourself the Following Questions:
- When my child says he can't do a task, how quickly do I jump in to help him?
- Is it possible I've sent the message that I think he can't do these tasks?

What Can You Do?
- Help your child know that *you* know he's capable.
- Build on what he already knows.

- Use the phrase, "I can help you by teaching you how."

It can be difficult to find the line between being a caring, sensitive parent and helping your child so much he begins to feel incapable. It's helpful to listen to what your child tells you through his actions and words. Sometimes when it appears your child needs you more, it may actually mean he needs you less in different ways. In other words, he needs you to let him try more things on his own so he sees that you know he can do them. You can be there as a guide, but not doing the task for him.

Dan Gartrell

Dan Gartrell, an emeritus professor of early childhood and foundations of education at Bemidji State University in northern Minnesota, also believes, like Dreikurs, that children don't aim to "be bad," but rather they have mistaken behaviors. In an article printed in *Young Children* in July 1995, Gartrell stated that there are three categories of mistaken behaviors: experimentation, socially influenced, and strong needs.

Mistaken Behaviors, Dan Gartrell, 1995

Experimentation

Socially Influenced

Strong Needs

Experimentation

Any behavior that's done by a child with the intent of experimenting falls into this category. A toddler who drives a toy truck around the house and bumps it into walls isn't trying to harm the walls; rather, she's trying to see what will happen. A four-year-old who's playing with her glass of water at the kitchen table and gradually tipping it over is also not trying to harm anything. She's simply trying to see if the water will spill out and, if so, how far will she need to tip it to make it happen. Children are truly scientists at heart so they're constantly experimenting.

Children are truly scientists at heart so they're constantly experimenting.

Although this is normal behavior for children, it doesn't mean the child should be allowed to continue the behavior. However, you want to make sure your child understands that you see her perspective in what she's doing. "I can see that you're trying to see if that water will spill. The glass needs to stay upright during dinner. Perhaps when you take your bath later you can take some cups in so you can try this in the bathtub where water belongs." Your child then understands that the action isn't okay at the table, but it could be done somewhere else at a different time. Some children might continue to tip their glass even after you've had this conversation with them. At that time, the glass may simply need to be taken away during the meal. This doesn't need to be done in an angry matter. You can simply say, "It seems hard for you to use this glass the way it's meant to be used. I will put it over here for you so it's not tempting." This isn't a punishment, but rather a logical consequence for tipping the glass after she had already been told not to.

When navigating experimentation behaviors, remember that most of the time these actions are very normal and are truly a sign that your child is interested in learning more about the world. It's important to keep that curiosity alive. The approach will be gentle and understanding while still guiding her to more acceptable behavior in that moment and explaining a more appropriate time for her to continue that behavior later.

Ask Yourself the Following Questions:

- Does my child seem genuinely engaged in what she's doing when she's exhibiting these behaviors or taking part in these actions?

What Can You Do?

- Tell your child what she can do instead.
- Don't reprimand or punish your child for these actions.
- Appreciate her curiosity, but still teach what's okay and what isn't okay.

Socially Influenced

Socially influenced behavior is usually behavior that's been picked up from peers, but it can sometimes come from the media. Examples of these behaviors are when your child might suddenly use potty talk or talk back to you. The behaviors shouldn't be allowed; however, understanding that your child is likely repeating something she heard recently helps you know how to address the situation. An honest and open conversation with her is often all that's needed. You could say, "I understand you heard this at school. It might be okay at Mandi's house, but those aren't words that are allowed at our house." If you find that there are repeated phrases that are unacceptable coming from specific television shows, it's likely time to remove that show as an option for viewing by your child.

> *Understanding that your child is likely repeating something she heard recently helps you know how to address the situation.*

Ask Yourself the Following Questions:

- Where might my child have heard this?

- Does my child think these behaviors or words are okay to use at home?

What Can You Do?

- Let your child know you understand she learned the behavior or language from a friend, TV, or school, but that it's not acceptable at your house.

- Decide if you want the sources of these behaviors or words to be a part of your child's life, and if not, decide how you can eliminate them or keep them to a minimum.

Strong Needs

Strong-needs behavior typically appears to be somewhat out of control and disconnected, such as an inability to follow directions or to harm other children with little remorse. This child may not be getting his basic needs met (Maslow's Hierarchy of Needs) or he may not have established a trust for himself or his caregivers in his earliest years (Erikson's developmental stages). Until this child's most basic needs are met, or the lack of trust in himself and the world around him is addressed, it will be very difficult, if not impossible, to move forward with any form of teaching in the academic and the social-emotional sense.

Ask Yourself the Following Questions:

- Is it possible my child isn't getting his most basic needs met, and if so, what needs aren't being met?

- Is it possible my child doesn't trust himself or the world around him?

What Can You Do?

- Seek out professional resources for your child.

- If you feel you aren't able to provide basic needs for your child, you can contact local social service agencies to see what resources they might have available to you and your child.

- If you feel you're providing the basic needs for your child and have worked to build trust, but the behavior still seems out of the ordinary, you can see if your child's pediatrician has any recommendations for therapists or child psychologists in your area.

- You can also check in with your child's school district to see what resources it offers.

- Provide the child with an abundance of encouragement and patience.

Although Dreikurs's and Gartrell's theories provide us with great insight into the root of children's behaviors, they're incomplete without the addition of three other causes of negative behavior: physical, social, and intellectual needs.

Physical Needs

All children have a need to move their bodies. With some children, this is more noticeable than it is in others. Unfortunately, many schools aren't organized in a way that's very conducive to allowing children to move throughout their day or even while they work. I've been very fortunate to teach in a couple different outdoor-based schools over the course of my career. Most of the time, the children in these programs are very successful, mainly because they're getting their physical activity needs met by getting fresh air and moving their bodies. The children are able to run, jump, dance, lift, pull, and more during their day.

Many years ago there was a child, Chase, who attended a preschool I worked at. Although I was not his teacher, I did observe him throughout the year and it was obvious Chase had an abundance of energy. It took a great deal of effort for the teachers to keep up with him, but he thrived in the program.

However, Chase was heading to kindergarten the following year. His teachers knew that most schools wouldn't be able to provide the level of physical activity that his preschool was able to offer for him. They worried how he would handle the transition to kindergarten. They feared he would be pegged as a "bad kid" and subsequently suffer socially, academically, and emotionally. The teachers met with Chase's mom about their concerns. They knew holding him back a year wasn't an option, as he was more than ready for most aspects of kindergarten. Chase's mom appreciated the teachers' concerns and was well aware of his need to move. She felt confident that with some planning and creativity, she would be able to help Chase with this transition.

The following fall, when I was home on maternity leave with my son, we would often take a walk in the morning. As we did this, Chase and his mom biked past us. Chase's mom had two younger children who sat in a Burley bike trailer as she and Chase biked. They were biking to school. I quickly realized which school they had chosen: a school in the city that was known for high levels of experiential learning. The school, however, was not all that close to Chase's house. His mom knew that this morning bike ride to school would be exactly what Chase needed to help him focus during the day. It was obvious it wasn't easy for this mom of three to get out the door on a bike every morning to help her son, but she was willing and able to make this sacrifice for him.

If your child struggles in school, one of the first things you should look at is if he's getting his physical activity needs met.

physical activity

I, too, have a son with great physical activity needs. I aim for him to be out the door at least twenty minutes before the bus

79

comes so that he has time to play outside throwing the football or shooting hoops before the bus comes. I know this physical activity helps my son, and even though it requires us to plan ahead more than we might otherwise, it's worth it.

If your child struggles in school, one of the first things you should look at is if he's getting his physical activity needs met. Many schools are moving away from offering recess every day since they have such strong academic standards that need to be met. This is a mistake. Children end up suffering academically if they lose out on this very important time, not only to get fresh air, but also to be physically active. In his 2005 book, *Last Child in the Woods*, Richard Louv discusses the issues children in today's culture face since they have limited time outdoors being active in unconstrained ways, at home and at school. If your child doesn't have an opportunity to be physically active at school, discuss this concern with your child's teacher and principal. If you can't change the situation at school, find ways for your child to get his physical activity needs met before and after school. Ideally, children should have physical activity opportunities for all: before school, during school, and after school.

Some schools allow their students to stand during class or sit on an exercise ball as they do their work in place of a regular chair. This can be very helpful for many children. It's been found that the use of these balls can bring calmness and focus in the classroom (B. Pytel, 2007 and Schilling et al, 2003), which likely, in turn, would boost academics. To an outsider, it may look like a chaotic classroom and certainly not what many adults experienced when they were children. However, this was not as needed twenty to thirty years ago because many children at that time had numerous opportunities to be physically active before, during, and after school. The needs were met more naturally at that time.

Sometimes the physical needs are unrelated to the demand for more physical activity, but they're related to simply having basic physical needs going unrecognized. Young children often don't realize, for example, that they don't feel well or are getting hot. When a child doesn't recognize that these things are happening, he'll begin to exhibit negative behaviors. Eric was a child in my class years ago who often exhibited negative behaviors soon after we came in from outside, especially in the winter months. After a couple weeks of trying different techniques, I realized that Eric had long underwear on under his jeans. I wondered if Eric was getting hot in the classroom wearing both jeans and long underwear. Once I made this realization, I had Eric take his long underwear off from underneath his jeans once we came in from outside. I noticed an immediate difference in Eric's behavior. He had been hot, but he was unable to articulate this. It created a disregulation in his body, which led to his negative behaviors. Many times some of the most basic things should be examined when your child is exhibiting challenging behaviors.

Ask Yourself the Following Questions:

- Does my child tend to need a great deal of physical exercise?

- What differences do I see in my child when he does get the physical exercise he needs, even if his physical exercise needs don't seem significant?

- Are other basic needs going unrecognized?

  - Is my child getting sick?

- Is he too hot right now?

- Is he cold?

- Is he uncomfortable in other ways?

- Does he need to use the bathroom?

- Is my child hungry?

- Is my child tired and in need of more sleep?

What Can You Do?

- Seek out programs that allow for and embrace physical activity.

- Be sure to find time during your child's day for him to get the physical activity he needs.

- According to the American Academy of Pediatrics, in 2011, children should have at least sixty minutes of physical activity each day. This can be done in increments or all at once. It's important to know, though, that many children will need far more than sixty minutes each day.

- Be an advocate for your child in school to help find ways that physical activity can be built into his day to help him be successful.

- Be in tune to your child's needs.

- Be aware of when he usually needs to eat, sleep, use the toilet, et cetera.

- As he gets older, gradually begin to teach him how to be in tune to his own needs as well.

Social Needs

When children are toddlers and preschoolers, they don't always have the social skills to interact successfully with their peers. They continue to be egocentric in these years and need much guidance through play and interactions with their peers. Unfortunately, in some settings, what is typical behavior for toddlers and preschoolers can be viewed as troublesome behavior by caregivers. Ronin was a rambunctious three-year-old in my class more than ten years ago. He loved life and was so excited to be with other children. Ronin was an only child and had very little experience interacting with his peers. Whenever he entered a group of children playing, there was drama, usually involving Ronin knocking over the other children's block structures. Although this can be difficult to manage in a preschool classroom, it's very common.

Unfortunately, in some settings, what is typical behavior for toddlers and preschoolers can be viewed as troublesome behavior by caregivers.

Ronin simply didn't have the skills to know how to interact with other children. He was attempting to play with these children by knocking over their block structures. Even though the reactions from the other children quickly turned negative, Ronin didn't really mind. He was just glad to be interacting.

In many classrooms Ronin may have been put on a behavior chart or pegged as a "bad kid." I knew, however, that I simply needed to do some social skills training with him. The main goal in toddler and preschool programs should be to help children learn these skills. It's ideal if the parents are teaching these skills at home as well, but it shouldn't be expected that all children have perfect social skills at these ages. Find programs for this age group that recognize children are still in the process of learning these skills and won't punish or shame a child for imperfections in these areas. Instead, these should be viewed as opportunities for learning. This is critical to helping your child maintain positive self-confidence. With help, Ronin eventually learned positive social skills, and within the year he had even formed a couple friendships.

Ask Yourself the Following Questions:

- Does my child have the skills needed to interact socially without adult assistance? If not,
  - How can I begin to teach him this?
  - What adults will I need on board to help my child learn social skills?
- When my child disrupts the play of other children, what is he trying to gain at this time?

What Can You Do?

- Understand that your child is simply trying to interact with his peers, but he will need guidance on how to do so.
- Coach your child through social interactions until he has stronger social skills.
- Set your child up for success by starting small. For example, start with play time with one or two other children before placing the child in large groups of children.
- Be patient.

Intellectual Needs

Oftentimes, what looks like misbehavior in children is actually a sign that the child isn't being intellectually stimulated enough, especially if it's in a child-care or school setting. When children are young (under five), this doesn't mean academics (in the narrow sense) need to be increased, but it might mean you need to provide more challenging toys or games. Perhaps your child has grown too comfortable in the environment and switching some of the things in this environment will help stimulate his brain again. For older children, it's possible that academics need to be boosted. The child may be ready to perform above grade level, but she isn't being provided that opportunity. Parents and teachers need to look at what might be able to be supplemented for the child so she can be intellectually stimulated to keep her brain growing and developing to its potential.

Oftentimes, what looks like misbehavior in children is actually a sign that the child isn't being intellectually stimulated enough, especially if it's in a child-care or school setting.

There are also times when your child might act up in class because the material is too difficult for him. Rather than being bored, he feels lost and incompetent. He might begin to show attention-getting behavior to distract his classmates. In this case, he may be ready for some supplementation. It's important to address this as soon as possible, so the child doesn't fall too far behind and lose his desire to learn. Thinking back to Vygotsky's ZPD, you might consider ways to scaffold what the child already knows to stretch him to what he's struggling to understand in school. An adult or older child or peer would be beneficial to help during this time.

It's critical for you to discuss either of these issues with the teacher so you understand where your child is intellectually. Assessing this can take time, but it's worth the extra effort because it will help you understand your child's perspective and developmental growth.

Ask Yourself the Following Questions:

- Is my child being stimulated enough or is the material or environment too challenging for my child?

- Could the school help with this, or do I need to look at this only at home?

- Do I need to look to outside resources at this time, such as different schooling options, gifted and talented programming, special education programming, et cetera?

What Can You Do?

- Meet with your child's teachers to see what their perspective is.

- Make a plan with your child's teachers and school to assist with this issue.

- Seek out further resources for your child if needed.

How Did Asia Use the Above Information to Help Javan?

At the beginning of this chapter, you were introduced to ten-year-old Javan and his mom, Asia. Javan had been struggling at home with following through with any requests his parents made of him unless they stayed with him while he completed the task. He had also begun to be disruptive at school. Asia decided to meet with Javan's teacher to delve more deeply into why he was behaving the way he was at school. In the meeting, Asia learned that Javan hadn't been turning in his homework although he always told Asia he had. The teacher said she noticed that Javan often looked over his classmates's shoulders during tests and other work times. She was beginning to wonder if the material was too difficult for him. When Asia asked Javan about his homework, he became very defensive. She told him how she struggled with her homework as a child and sometimes would hide it or say she already did it. Javan's shoulders relaxed, and he admitted that this was what he was doing too. The lack of getting his intellectual needs met was causing his negative behavior at school. His disregard for his homework was caused from feelings of inadequacy. He felt he was likely not going to be able to do it, so he wouldn't even bother trying. Luckily, the school was able to provide Javan with additional help. Within a couple months, these negative behaviors were eliminated.

Javan's parents were thrilled that the school issues were able to be addressed; however, they still had concerns about his behavior at home. When we discussed the various moments he was likely to exhibit these actions, it became obvious that these were attention-getting behaviors. When Javan put off doing his chores, his parents usually spent time talking to him about this until they simply stood right there until he did the task, therefore providing him with attention. Javan's parents decided to have some focused one-on-one time with him alone without the distractions of their younger children. This special time helped improve Javan's attitude almost instantly.

The above information offers you a framework for understanding your child's behaviors. You need to set limits and be there for your child as a guide, but you also need to understand different approaches are necessary, depending on what the mistaken goal or behavior is. Most of the time, children are unaware of the true reason or goals for their behaviors. It happens subconsciously. Because of this, there is no need to explain to them that you know their behavior is attention getting or revenge seeking, for example. These terms are for our understanding alone. Table 3 offers a summary of these ten causes along with what you can do to aid in these situations and what you should avoid.

Most of the time, children are unaware of the true reason or goals for their behaviors.

TABLE 3

Summary of Goals for or Causes of Children's Negative Behaviors		
	What You Can Do	**What to Avoid Doing**
Attention getting • To get attention	• Give attention at other times when your child isn't showing attention-getting behavior.	• Avoid giving your child attention for the ill behavior at the time.
Power seeking • To gain power	• Look at what ways your child can have more power in other parts of his life. • Acknowledge that your child would like to be in control: "You wish you could…" • Remain calm.	• Don't engage in the power struggle. • Don't give in to your child.
Revenge Seeking • To get revenge	• You may not be able to do a lot verbally in the moment, as the child might be too out of control to actually hear you. • Physically, you may need to restrain your child so he can't hurt you or anyone else. • Work to help your child see that you're on his side in life.	• Avoid acknowledging that your feelings might be hurt by the child's actions or words. • Avoid stooping to the child's level by: retaliating, yelling, imitating, or hitting the child.
Displaying Inadequacy • Feeling inadequate	• Have confidence in your child: "I know you can do this. You're so strong and capable." • Reserve time for her growing skills. • Offer words of encouragement, such as, "I can help you by teaching you how to help yourself."	• Avoid rescuing and doing things for your child that she can do for herself. • Downplay mistakes.

Summary of Goals for or Causes of Children's Negative Behaviors

	What You Can Do	What to Avoid Doing
Experimentation • To see what will happen	• Show your child what she *can* do instead.	• Don't punish or reprimand your child for the behavior.
Socially Influenced • Heard words or saw behavior from friends, at school, or from media	• Explain that you understood she recently heard or saw this, but that it's not OK in your house.	• Don't get overly upset or excited about this, as it may only cause the behavior to happen more often.
Strong Needs • Isn't getting basic needs met • Hasn't learned basic trust in self and world	• Seek out resources so your child can get her basic needs met. • Provide your child with an abundance of encouragement and patience.	• Avoid harsh punishments and reprimands.
Physical Needs • Needs more physical activity • Not getting basic physical needs met in the moment	• Find ways for your child to use his physical energy in positive ways. • Be thoughtful in planning your day so the child has opportunities to move. • Be aware of when your child needs food, sleep, the bathroom, etc. or when he's getting sick. • Gradually begin to teach your child to recognize what these behaviors mean.	• Eliminate the use of TV and other media for long periods of time. • Be patient and avoid punishment.
Social Needs • Lacking social skills for situation	• Be available to coach your child through social situations. • Acknowledge that you know your child is hoping to play and connect with the other children.	• Don't punish or reprimand for these behaviors.

Summary of Goals for or Causes of Children's Negative Behaviors		
	What You Can Do	What to Avoid Doing
Intellectual Needs • Not being intellectually stimulated enough • Material is too difficult	• If your child needs more stimulation, find things for her to do at home, school, or elsewhere. • If the school work is too much for your child, be an advocate for her at her school so she can get the resources she needs. • Get to know your child's teachers and become active in her school to aid in the home/school connection.	• Avoid punishing or reprimanding your child for behavior that happens at school. Allow the school to cover this on their end.

Discipline or Punishment?

Often the words discipline and punishment are used interchangeably; however, I see these as two very different approaches in raising children. Discipline comes from the Latin word *disciplinaire*, which means "to teach." When I think of the word "teach," I immediately think of giving instruction. When one gives instruction to another person, for that person to actually learn, it needs to be done with patience, understanding, and respect. Punishment, on the other hand, usually involves pain, suffering, or loss inflicted by another person for an offense. The person being punished may stop the behavior that led to the punishment, but the root of the issue likely hasn't been addressed.

The reason for sharing the information in this chapter is to provide you with a means of understanding your child's negative behaviors, so you can react to him with patience, understanding, and respect. This sets you on the path to teaching, rather than punishing for negative behaviors. When you choose this route, you'll have a closer, connected relationship with your child through this journey. I will discuss this further in chapter five.

CHAPTER FOUR
Who Is This Child?

My son, Ian, my firstborn, came into the world with a strong presence. He arrived three and a half weeks early, likely worried he was missing out on something wonderful in this world. April 12 was the day my family had planned to hold my baby shower. What child wants to miss his own party? Of course, what Ian didn't know is that by arriving on April 12, we would ALL miss out on the shower.

At one point in the hospital, Ian was crying so loudly the nurses asked me if I wanted a break. The delivery had taken a bit out of me, so having some alone time sounded appealing. It couldn't have been more than thirty minutes later when they brought Ian back to me and said he was waking the other babies. To be honest, Ian's cry didn't seem out of the ordinary to me because I hadn't spent much time with newborns prior to his birth. I thought to myself, "Isn't this what they all do?"

Ian's crying continued for months. We found ways to comfort him, but it was usually a balancing act (literally, balancing on an exercise ball while bouncing up and down). For a while, I avoided situations where I would be with other parents who had infants because they didn't seem to share in my struggles. My husband and I wondered if there was something wrong with us as parents or if there was something wrong with our son. We felt extremely helpless.

As a result, my husband and I visited Ian's doctor on numerous occasions and even sought second opinions. I tried cutting foods out of my diet in case my breastmilk was irritating his digestive system. We tried a special formula for severely allergic children. We also tried antireflux medicine. None of these changed things for Ian. He still cried loud and often.

My husband and I wondered if there was something wrong with us as parents or if there was something wrong with our son. We felt extremely helpless.

Finally, at one doctor's visit as I was trying to convince the doctor that there must be something wrong with my son, she looked at me and said, "Have you heard of temperament?" Of course I had. I was a teacher! I had worked with numerous children, and they were all so different from each other. The doctor put her hand on my shoulder and said, "There's nothing wrong with your son. He's just like this. He has strong opinions and wants them known. He'll likely always have this intensity to him." I think deep down this is what I was afraid of the whole time. Of course, I wanted him to be healthy, but I figured if something was wrong it would be something they could fix pretty easily. Not temperament, though. That sounded rather permanent.

I began to have terrible thoughts, such as "This isn't the baby I thought I'd have!" I had imagined a baby who would happily join along in the life that my husband and I had already started, who would fall asleep peacefully when he was ready for sleep, and who would whimper when he needed something. Looking back now, I realize that I was foolish to think that a "perfect" baby even existed. More so, it was unfair to Ian for me to have this expectation of him, as it was clearly unrealistic. Unfortunately, it took me a couple years to fully come to these realizations.

Knowing the importance of attachment, my husband and I hung in there. We held Ian when he needed to be held, even though it was more often than not. We bounced on the exercise ball gently for all hours as we held him, knowing he needed the rhythm to be soothed. We adopted the idea that "if we give him what he needs when he needs it, he won't always need it." My husband and I took turns often with Ian to make sure we were able to keep our patience. We enlisted the help of family at times to give us both a break when we felt it was needed. All of these things helped us to create a closeness and connection to Ian despite his challenging baby and toddler years. However, there was still a part of me who mourned the loss of the child I thought I was going to have. Life often throws us surprises. Some of these surprises are stressful, and we wonder how we'll survive them. Others end up changing our lives forever in such wonderful ways. Life with Ian has been both of these things for my husband and me.

There were days with my son that I wondered how we were

going to survive raising him. His temper tantrums could last thirty to sixty minutes with kicking and screaming. I knew he couldn't be happy acting this way. I knew I was doing what felt like the right thing, but none of it seemed to be working.

I thought back to the doctor's words about temperament. I wondered, "How much do I really know about this?" It wasn't something I spent a lot of time learning about in college. Although I had worked with many children, they typically acted different for me than they did for their parents. Hence, as a teacher I didn't always see the full temperament traits in the children. I decided I needed to learn more about this subject.

Mary Sheedy Kurcinka has a book on temperament called *The Spirited Child*. I had heard of this book numerous times from the parents of the children I taught, but I had always been very hesitant to read it. I had heard the label "spirited child" from so many parents, and the truth is I dislike labels for children. They often put unnecessary judgments on a child. However, since I felt overwhelmed with my own son, I figured the book was worth a read. In writing her book, Kurcinka sought to provide a unique resource for parents—one that was positive and offered hopefulness to parents. She succeeded in both.

What I learned from Kurcinka's book ended up being one of the greatest gifts to my family. I not only gained a greater understanding of Ian, but also a greater understanding of myself as a person, a mom, and a teacher. I've always felt that Ian and I have had a strong relationship; however, it's grown tenfold since I spent time learning more about his temperament. Overall, it helped us understand his behaviors and reactions better. We gained the tools needed to navigate his temperament in a way that's helped him continue to grow in his confidence and in his ability to assess his own strong reactions to the situations he encounters.

Within Kurcinka's book, there are temperament assessments that you can use to help determine where your child falls in areas such as intensity, regularity, persistence, sensitivity, adaptability, and more. She then provides vignettes and suggestions on how to approach these various temperament traits. I'm not going to try to rewrite something that's already written so well, but I encourage you to read her book if you want more information on temperament than I provide here.

Through the years, I've learned that infant fussiness is not necessarily a predictor of later temperament. In fact, pediatrician Harvey Karp discusses the idea of the fourth trimester in his book, *Happiest Baby on the Block*: "Once born, many babies are able to adapt to the world outside the womb. Some, however, have a hard time adjusting, are stressed, and end up crying inconsolably for hours on end" (Karp, 2003). My son was one of these babies who didn't adjust to life outside of the womb very well.

As Ian's parents, we still see signs of intensity in him; however, as he's grown older, it has come out in different ways. He rarely loses control physically or emotionally anymore. Yet, when he plays sports and works on schoolwork, he puts his intensity toward working hard and pushing himself. Most people who know my son well now are shocked to hear we ever had any struggles with him with emotional outbursts and inflexibility. To them, he's extremely in control and adaptable. Children's temperament evolves over time, both in response to their internal makeup and the environments that shape them.

Below I will review the five most common temperament traits I receive questions and concerns about. It's not that the other traits aren't important; however, they seem to cause less concern and stress in parents than the five I will discuss here.

Temperament Traits

All children are different. They have different characteristics that make them who they are. Because of this, I've never believed there's only one prescribed way to react to a child. There are too many variables for it to be that simple. How you react depends on the situation, the child's temperament, and WHY the child is acting the way he's acting. We've already addressed the latter in the previous chapter, so let's take a look at some of the temperament traits your child may possess at this time and learn how you can best react to these traits.

When discussing each trait, I will first go through basic characteristics of this trait and then how you can begin to help your child learn how to manage the trait(s). It's important that these traits aren't used as excuses for behavior but as an understanding. It's beneficial for children to learn the important skills of knowing they can have some control. When your child is younger, it's your job as the parent to understand who he is so you can best meet his needs. However, as he gets older (beginning around four years old), your job switches from teaching yourself to teaching *him* to understand himself, so he's able to manage these various qualities. This is a process. Much of your parenting through the years will include teaching these skills.

> ### Five Prominent Temperament Traits
>
> *Adaptability*
>
> *Persistence*
>
> *Perceptiveness/Distractibility*
>
> *Sensitivity*
>
> *Intensity*

Adaptability

Characteristics of Adaptability in Children

Adaptability is how easily a child adapts to changes in routines and schedules. Some children can take change in stride, while others struggle with it a great deal. It's important to give all children a warning when change will be approaching, but it's even more important for a child who's slower to adapt. When children are young (approximately age three and under), it's helpful to limit the number of transitions that take place in a day, if possible.

Robby, age two, attends a child-care center three days a week. When he arrives at the center in the morning, all the children gather in a small play area until more children and teachers arrive. After about an hour, Robby moves into his regular classroom with his classmates and teachers. Around three in the afternoon each day, all the children move into the smaller play area again. Robby has a very difficult time with these changes.

He's sad to leave his dad each morning, but he eventually finds comfort in one of the teachers that he's with for the first hour. When it's time to move to his regular classroom, he doesn't want to leave behind the adult he just found comfort in. As a result, Robby is very unsettled at school.

Robby's parents have wondered if something is wrong with him because he struggles with transitions. However, the more they learn about their son, the more they realize they need to make a new plan for daycare. They realize how confusing these changes must be not only to a small child, but also even more so to a child who is slow to adapt.

Many children who are slow to adapt can greatly benefit from using picture calendars or schedules to help them know what's coming next. Adults can simply draw pictures of the day's schedule or use photographs for this. In Robby's case, the teachers could take photos of him arriving at school, playing in the first room, moving to his regular classroom, playing in his regular classroom, and then moving to the original room again. This could be made into a small book for Robby to review before school and during his day.

A visual schedule may be enough to comfort Robby, but more may be needed. It's possible the schedule won't end up working for Robby. His parents and teachers won't know until they try some new approaches to see what, if anything, works. Essentially, this environment may not be the best fit for Robby's temperament. Robby likely, since he's slower to adapt, would benefit from an environment with consistent teachers and limited transitions.

If your child is slower to adapt, he'll need more time to adjust to new schedules and routines. When switching child-care centers or schools, it's helpful to have him spend some time in the new setting before you leave him there for the first time. Your child may simply need time to observe before engaging and this should be accepted. It's beneficial if you acknowledge this, but don't overemphasize it to others, especially in front of your child. Doing so can make your child feel like it's an expectation for him to stand back at first. The reality is that

When the slower-to-adapt child watches before getting involved, he's often assessing the circumstances to determine if it's safe.

you never know what experiences will draw your child out, so you should keep an open mind. When the slower-to-adapt child watches before getting involved, he's often assessing the circumstances to determine if it's safe. He will be less likely to get caught up in negative peer influences because he'll be taking the time to step back and evaluate the situation.

Helping Your Child Understand Adaptability

If your child is slower to adapt, she likely won't need much coaching beyond your patience with this temperament trait. You might struggle more with this characteristic than your child does. It can be difficult to see your child missing out on activities. However, much of the time the child who is slower to adapt doesn't view life like this at all. This is how she first takes things in: looks around, watches, and gets involved when she's ready. Sometimes your child might feel frustrated about not connecting with friends at a new school or say she doesn't like something after only going to it a few times. It's beneficial to remind your child that change often doesn't come naturally to her, but with time it will get easier. Helping her understand her traits and how other people might be interpreting her actions is critical for her personal growth and development. As your child gets older, she'll gradually adjust accordingly to different situations.

Sometimes parents need to give children a gentle nudge. Last summer, a woman named Renee called me right before her five-and-a-half-year-old child's class was about to start. It was the first day of an eight-day class at the summer program I direct. Renee told me that her daughter, Shelby, was saying she didn't want to come to class. Shelby didn't like new situations and was afraid to come. I remembered meeting Renee and Shelby at the open house we had the month prior to this. Shelby stood back during that visit. However, I remember talking at great length with Renee and showing Shelby around the school. During the phone call, Renee said she didn't know what to do. I asked her if she wanted Shelby to stay for the class. Renee said yes, but she worried about leaving her with us when she might cry. I explained to Renee that it was her choice, but we would be more than ready to have Shelby stay with us even if she was crying. I told her that Shelby would likely settle down soon after Renee left. Renee and I talked a few more minutes. Before hanging up, Renee thanked me for listening and said she would see me soon.

When Renee and Shelby arrived, I could tell Shelby had been crying. I greeted her quietly and told her how happy I was to see her. Renee walked her over to where the other kids were gathering. I pointed out a flower that was growing right where we were meeting, which drew Shelby's attention away from being sad momentarily. Renee bent down to Shelby and told her that she would see her after class. Shelby began to whimper, but she quickly stopped when I pointed out another flower near where we were waiting. During class, Shelby had moments where she chose not to be involved, but she stayed nearby. She gradually decided to get more involved as the class days went on. At the end of the session, Renee thanked me for guiding her through that first day. She said she was glad that Shelby had the opportunity to have success with being left somewhere. Renee realized that Shelby might always be slower to warm up. She knew these moments of success were likely helping her to avoid overanxious feelings in future situations. If Renee hadn't given Shelby this gentle nudge, it would have confirmed Shelby's belief that she should be fearful of new situations.

Summary of Tips for Parenting Your Slower-to-Adapt Child

- Give your child a warning when change is about to happen.
- Limit the number of transitions, when possible, especially for children three and younger.
- Use photo books to ease transitions.
- Be patient with your child as she adapts to change.
- Take time to bring your child to visit a new school before the school year begins.
- Let your child know you have confidence in her.
- Provide a gentle nudge when you think she's ready.

Persistence

Characteristics of Persistence in Children

A persistent child is very determined and strong. This is the child who can't seem to take no for an answer. The persistent child pushes when other children typically don't. She demands when others don't demand. It's extremely hard to ignore or distract a persistent child. All children need to feel in control and have power; however, this feeling is critical with a persistent child.

All children need to feel in control and have power; however, this feeling is critical with a persistent child.

Selena has always loved animals. Since she was three years old, she has been asking her parents to buy her a pet of her own. Her parents are not sure if they're ready for a pet, so they keep putting her off. Selena asks every day, multiple times during the day, when she can have a pet. Her parents have explained that they won't be able to have a furry pet due to her brother's allergies. Selena simply says, "I can get another pet then." They have also told her they aren't sure if they have room for a pet because they live in a fairly small apartment. Selena always has a creative response about how she could make it work even in their small apartment. When her parents tell her that she needs money to pay for her pet, she's quick to explain how she'll make money by walking the neighbors' dogs a couple times each week. She's not giving up on this hope to own a pet, and Selena's parents are constantly frustrated by her persistence.

Persistence is a very admirable trait. Truly, it's hard to argue with someone who is so committed to her goals. Selena's parents realized how frustrated she must be feeling, so they told her that she needed to research what kind of animals don't have fur and can live in small spaces. They also asked her to find out the cost not only of the animal, but also of the habitat it would need along with the other needed supplies: food, bedding, et cetera. Selena then presented this information to her parents so they could discuss the subject further. They knew this would provide Selena with some feelings of power and buy them some time to determine themselves what kind of animals they would be open to having, if any. In the end, their answer was still no, but at least Selena felt like they had given her a fair shot at this idea. She was then more willing to accept this answer.

The type of power that Selena's parents gave her is the *right* kind of power. However, if they waver on their final decision that she can't have a pet at this time and give in to her request, it will lead to her having the *wrong* kind of power and control. We still need to be the adult in the relationship, and although Selena might be able to argue her way out of the final decision, that doesn't mean she should be allowed to do so. When parenting your persistent child, it's very important that you mean what you say and stick with it. If you go back on your word, even once, your persistent child will remember this and continue to test her theory that "I don't think they really mean what they say." I will go into more detail about the *right* and *wrong* kind of power in chapter six. Power is a driving force for the persistent child.

Helping Your Child Understand Persistence

The need for power in your persistent child can affect her social interactions in negative ways. She may feel the need to always be in control of the play with her friends. This can create negative feelings with the other children, with them thinking your child doesn't listen to them or respect them. Your child may need social coaching more than other children to help her understand why her friends might sometimes feel overwhelmed by her. In reality, this isn't something you can change for your child unless *she* begins to see that change might be needed. If your child is more demanding with her friends and thinks her ideas are the best, she'll gradually begin losing friends. Until this happens, she may not see that she needs to change her approach. You need to model for your child what is expected in peer relationships. If you allow her to overpower you and her persistence pays off at home, she will learn that this works for her. As she spends more time interacting with people beyond her family, she will be alarmed to see that most people won't give in to her demands and may actually avoid her abrasive behavior.

Summary of Tips for Parenting Your Persistent Child

- Provide situations for your child to feel power and control, but make sure it's the *right* kind of power and control.

- Be consistent.

- When you say "no," stick with it.

- Help your child to see that her persistence is something to be admired, but others may perceive it as being pushy and abrasive.

- Coach your child through social situations as needed.

Perceptiveness/Distractibility

Characteristics of Perceptiveness/Distractibility in Children

A perceptive child is often easily distracted. Our family jokes that the way my two children came into this world is very fitting with their temperaments. Ian's intensity usually involves him not wanting to miss out on anything. Although he doesn't always jump in right away, he at least wants to know what's going on. I already told you that Ian entered the world early, likely not wanting to miss out on anything. Maya, my daughter, on the other hand, arrived a couple days late. She is very distractible because she notices everything. We joke that she likely had plans to be born sooner, but she simply got distracted on her way out. She probably noticed new areas in the womb that she hadn't yet explored.

If your child is very perceptive, she will benefit from being given only a couple directions at a time. Otherwise, she will likely be distracted by something else in the middle of all the directions. Pictures and written lists are extremely helpful for a child who falls in this category. For many months, we had issues with Maya getting to bed on time. She needed constant reminders about what she needed to do as she was getting ready for bed. I sat down with her to find out if she actually knew what was expected of her. She listed off ten things she needed to do to get ready for bed. Maya was five years old at the time, and I realized that ten things are quite a bit for a child this age to remember, especially one who is more perceptive.

I decided to create a list of these ten things that Maya could check off once she accomplished them. This provided her with a focus and made the goal seem more attainable. She didn't get a reward for doing these tasks, other than the joy of knowing she got them done.

Often, perceptiveness is interpreted as misbehavior or stalling. Sometimes it's the latter, but it usually means the child is so perceptive that she has difficulty focusing. Another aspect of perceptiveness is the intake of sounds and visuals. A child who's overly perceptive seems to hear and see everything and often is unsure which are the aspects she should be attending to. Sometimes it might appear like your child is ignoring you when you're talking to her. Again, she may simply be trying to figure out what sounds to attend to. You don't want to use this as an excuse for her lack of focus. Instead, provide her with tools to help her stay focused when needed, such as a visual list of tasks to be completed or limiting the amount of stimulation in the environment in these moments.

A child who's overly perceptive seems to hear and see everything and often is unsure which are the aspects she should be attending to.

Over the years, I've come to admire this trait in my daughter, although it does cause us to be late at times. I appreciate her ability to live in the moment. Hikes in nature and simple walks around our neighborhood could take hours as she stops to notice the smallest plants and other living creatures. Her sense of wonder is certainly fully alive and something we could all learn from.

Helping Your Child Understand Perceptiveness/Distractibility

Despite the admirable characteristics of a perceptive child, you will still need to provide your child with tools to manage the distractibility, so she'll be able to focus when needed. If your child is more perceptive or distractible, she can learn, as she gets older, to create her own to-do list as opposed to you continuing to create this list for her. Your child can also begin to learn what she needs to do to establish a focused environment when studying or reading. You can help your child think through what this space might look and feel like, and you can assist with helping the rest of the family support her need for fewer distractions. It's helpful for your child to understand her needs without it feeling like a limitation. For example, you might say, "It seems that it's easiest for you to get your homework done when you do it at the desk in the office rather than in the living room. Having that quiet space seems to help your brain work better." As your child gets older, she may not always need a quiet space to work. It's still important for her to know what these needs are and how to manage them.

Summary of Tips for Parenting Your Perceptive/Distractible Child

- Use pictures or written to-do lists to draw your child's focus in.

- Keep in mind that your child isn't trying to frustrate or ignore you.

- Eliminate stimulation in the environment when your child needs to focus.

- Have a separate area of the house where she can do her homework.

- Make a quieter classroom setting or desk in a location where there are limited distractions.

Sensitivity

Characteristics of Sensitivity in Children

There are a few different aspects of sensitivity, including a child who's sensitive to noises and bright lights, who's irritated by the way clothes feel, or who's emotionally delicate. Many parents will describe their sensitive child as someone who sees everything, feels everything, and smells everything. As a result, the senses quickly become overloaded and shut down.

Lin was a baby I knew a few years ago. She was the youngest child with three older siblings. Lin was fairly happy when she was home with just her family. However, as soon as people came over to the house or her family went out, Lin struggled. She was very fussy and would try to move her face away from everyone. Lin's mom was really confused since Lin was usually pretty happy. They noticed that Lin slept poorly on these nights as well. It became apparent that Lin was over-stimulated when she was around other people beyond her family. Lin's parents decided to hire a sitter for her when they had larger gatherings to go to. Sometimes Lin's mom would just stay home with her. As Lin got older, her parents gradually began to have more people over to their home. They started small, and as soon as they noticed Lin turning her face away from the visitors, they would bring her to a different room where it was quieter. Soon enough, Lin began to feel comfortable entering into these situations on her own because it was on her own terms. She could toddle out if she was done, assuming the adults in her presence allowed her to do this.

Having a child who is sensitive to noises, lights, people, and touch can be very challenging. It might mean missing out on things that the rest of your family is taking part in. It might mean changing how your household is set up and run. One family I worked with was astounded by the change they observed in their child once they decided to turn the TV off in their house during the day. It's not that the child was even watching TV, but she was hearing the noises from it and seeing the bright lights from it as she played. It hadn't occurred to them that this might be adding to her poor mood each day.

If your child is prone to overstimulation, it's helpful if you stay in tune to how your child's reacting to certain situations, so he can be removed or avoid these situations altogether. As your child gets older and has better coping skills, it's helpful to teach the child the cues that show he's getting over-stimulated. In other words, when he's had enough stimulation, he can begin to remove himself from the situation on his own.

Some sensitive children have issues with how their clothes feel. Your child may be irritated with the tag in his shirt, the line in his sock, or the tightness of his jeans. If these sensitivities appear out of nowhere with your child, it's more likely that he's feeling powerless in some way and is trying to feel in control again. This is a common occurrence after a child starts kindergarten. The child's in a new environment, having to sit through more teacher-led activities, and he is naturally feeling less in control. Kindergarten is a big change for many children. If you find that your child is suddenly struggling with clothing, allow her to choose her own clothing to eliminate the power struggle. It may not be a battle worth fighting, except for occasions that your child must wear something specific, such as a Cub Scout or soccer uniform.

When sensitivities to clothing seem to have been present

since birth, it's helpful to be extra patient with this. However, it will be valuable to gradually encourage your child to wear more types of clothing than she currently seems comfortable in. Allow your child to help pick out clothes when you're shopping. Occasionally, extreme sensitivities in children can be signs of underlying issues. If these strong sensitivities to clothing, textures, and stimulation feel extreme to you, check in with your child's teacher to see if she observes these characteristics in your child as well. I would also recommend mentioning these sensitivities to your child's doctor to see if additional resources are needed.

Some children are very emotionally delicate. They often feel the emotions of others, sometimes even before that person might feel the emotions herself. This is the child who cries when he sees other people crying, gets sad when he's being disciplined, even when it seems like it's being done in a respectful manner. This child is typically very sensitive to tone and will sense when adults may not like him.

Aaron has always been a very tender child. He loved to snuggle when he was a baby and even at age eight still hugs his teacher each morning when he arrives at school. When Aaron was younger, he would become very upset if he heard someone crying. In fact, many times he would begin to cry too, even if he didn't even know the person crying. Aaron's mom can gauge how stressed out she is by Aaron's behavior. If Aaron is grouchy and struggling to sleep, his mom knows *she* must be stressed. As soon as she finds ways to alleviate her stress, these behaviors in Aaron dissipate. All children benefit from having close, connected relationships with the adults in their lives. However, this is especially important for a child like Aaron. If he feels disconnected from the adults he spends time with, he will not only be less likely to perform at the level he's capable of and more likely to act out, but he also will simply shut down emotionally. When a child like Aaron spends time with adults who genuinely care about and appreciate him, he will flourish.

Many times, the emotionally sensitive child is capable of understanding others in a unique way. Aaron feels the emotions of others so easily and has a desire to connect with people who might be in need of encouragement. He's willing to put his own needs after theirs, knowing that will make the other person feel good.

Helping Your Child Understand Sensitivity

If your child is prone to overstimulation, it's important to model an understanding of what this looks and feels like. For example, you might say, "I can tell your brain must feel fuzzy right now. It's so noisy and bright in here. Let's step out to take a break and come back when we both feel ready." Your child will hear these words and begin to use them herself eventually. As your child gets older, starting at about five or six, it's important to talk more directly with her about these feelings of overstimulation. This will give her an opportunity to begin to recognize what this feels like and what situations may prompt this. This is empowering and teaches her how to cope with this somewhat challenging trait.

When looking for school programming for your child, take time to think about how stimulating the environment might be and if it will work for your child. If it's generally an environment of chaos, noise, and an abundance of materials, your child may not be able to think clearly. Instead, look for a program that's less chaotic and values simplicity.

If your child struggles with clothing sensitivities, understand that this is a real feeling to your child. She's not saying it's uncomfortable to annoy you, but because it truly bothers her. I was a child who was extremely irritated by how tags felt and how clothes fit in general. I'm sure my mom disliked shopping with me because nothing ever felt right. To this day, I still struggle with this. My son struggles with these same issues. Still, it can be frustrating to deal with as we're trying to get out the door and suddenly the shoe doesn't feel right or the jacket is slightly tight in one area. At these times, it's most beneficial if I can remain calm and explain to my son that I understand how it feels. As his coping skills are improving, he's now gradually getting more comfortable trying a wider variety of clothing. However, this will likely be something he deals with his whole life.

Sometimes it's the unknown emotions alone that can feel scary and cause stress for a child.

If your child is emotionally delicate, it's helpful for him to understand what his different feelings are called. Sometimes it's the unknown emotions alone that can feel scary and cause stress for a child. Sometimes very sensitive children have a high emotional intelligence. To read more on this subject, I recommend Daniel Goleman's book, *Emotional Intelligence*. An emotionally sensitive child can often sense how everyone in the room is feeling, and may take these feelings on himself. Whether someone is sad, or feels disappointed in him, it's important to let your child know that it's not his responsibility to take care of how others feel. Gradually, with coaching, he'll manage this easier on his own, but it will likely always be a work in progress.

Summary of Tips for Parenting Your Sensitive Child

Overstimulation

- Be patient.
- Avoid overstimulation when possible (keep lights and noises down).
- Protect your child's need for quiet.

Clothing Sensitivities

- Be patient.
- Allow your child to pick out her own clothes.
- Gradually build up her variety of clothing types.

Emotionally Sensitive

- Be in tune to your child's emotions and your own.
- Seek out other adults to be in her life who want to genuinely connect with her.
- Coach your child through her feelings.

Intensity

Characteristics of Intensity in Children

I mentioned my son Ian's intensity at the beginning of this chapter. Although he rates high in other categories too—persistence and sensitivity—it's the intensity that seems to prevail. As I've spent more time learning about intensity, I've come to acknowledge that I'm a fairly intense person as well. Many parents I've spent time working with recognize that this is the case for them too if their child is exhibiting behaviors that might be common in this trait.

An intense child often reacts strongly and loudly. When the child is mad, he's *really* mad. When he's sad, he's *really* sad. Oftentimes, it feels like this child moves from being happy and content to being very upset without much warning. This is the child who loses control, who screams, yells, hits, or kicks when upset. There's really no reasoning with a child when he's react-

Oftentimes, it feels like this child moves from being happy and content to being very upset without much warning.

ing in these ways. It's helpful to identify the cues: what the child's face or body looks like right before the intense reaction and what type of situations are more likely to lead the child in this direction. For example, if you know that every time you tell your child it's time to get ready for bed he begins to scream and cry, you can take measures before to help dissipate the intensity. If your child is young, it might be beneficial to use distraction. With older children, it might mean giving the child a hug as he's being told it's time to start getting ready for bed to dissolve some of his intense emotions that often arise in these moments.

An intense child seems to need more sleep than other children. You'll need to avoid overscheduling your intense child and sticking with consistent bedtimes so he can get enough sleep. This is true of all children, but the repercussions of lack of sleep are more pronounced with an intense child. Since the intense child's heart rate is often escalated, he's more likely to react by yelling, hitting, or kicking.

Although many of the characteristics of an intense child can be challenging, being intense is truly an admirable trait. Many very successful people are intense. When one has a goal and a passion for something, often intensity is needed to not only pursue it, but also to complete it.

Helping Your Child Understand Intensity

Early on, your child will need help regulating his emotions. The feelings for the sensitive child can be scary because of the intensity and range of emotions. The best way to help him in the beginning will be to learn what helps dissipate some of his intensity and what escalates it. This will take time, and much of it will be trial and error. Many parents find they end up giving into the child during these moments because they want the loud crying and screaming to stop. However, this won't benefit your child in the long run.

The next step will be modeling that you understand his feelings. By empathizing with him, he'll gradually learn to put words to these emotions. You, for instance, can say, "I can tell you're mad right now. You wish you could have that cookie." If you said no to the cookie, stick with the no, but let him know you understand he's mad. When you convey to your child that you understand what he wants, your child will feel respected and heard. It may not help much in the moment, but it's still planting a seed of consistency and understanding.

When your child is about four or five years old, he'll be ready to begin to regulate these emotions more on his own, especially if you've guided him early on in this area. I developed a tool, the Stages of Control, to aid in this teaching. This can be used for all children, but it was originally developed with the intense child in mind. I will be discussing the Stages of Control later in this chapter.

Summary of Tips for Parenting Your Intense Child
- Be patient.

- Learn what moments are more likely to lead to an intense reaction.

- Learn what your child's body language looks like as his intensity builds.

- Convey to your child that you understand he's upset.

- Help the child to bring his heart rate down.

Evaluate Further

Before reading further, take time to contemplate the following questions on temperament as it relates to your child.

1. **Do any of the above temperament traits describe my child? If so, which ones and how?**

2. **What observations have I recently made of my child regarding temperament?**

3. **What techniques have I found to be helpful with my slower-to-adapt, persistent, perceptive, sensitive, and/or intense child?**

Stages of Control

I developed a tool to help parents identify their child's feelings in challenging moments. These moments are stressful to both you as the parent and to the child, regardless of what circumstances created them. Stress in children can be defined as any moment where the heart begins to race or blood pressure goes up and the head might feel hot. It might be caused by something as simple as your child not getting his way, but it could be a bigger issue, such as the stress he might feel when he's lost someone he loves. Stress is somewhat of a loose term, but I think it's best left this way so we don't forget that stress can look like many things in your child.

Stress in children can be defined as any moment where the heart begins to race or blood pressure goes up and the head might feel hot.

The following describes three different Stages of Control: The Level Head, the Ticking Time Bomb, and The Explosion. The idea is that you can use this tool to first identify what these different levels look like for your child, so you can be ready for these situations. Once you've identified what these moments look like, you can begin to see how you might react according to each stage. The following describes each stage and what your child might be experiencing during these moments or how he might describe how he feels in these moments. Once you feel you have a handle on how this looks for your child and when he's old enough to understand this, you can begin to teach him about these different stages as well. He can then learn what he needs to do at each stage to take control of his stress.

Stages of Control

 ## *The Level Head*

- All is going well.
- There are no signs that something might go awry.
- Learning can happen during this time.
- This is a great time for family meetings.

 ## *the Ticking Time Bomb*

- Child is agitated.
- Child's heart is beating faster.
- Child's blood pressure is up.
- Adult caring for child begins to feels like s/he has to walk on eggshells.
- Whininess might begin.
- Arguing might happen.

- Child might describe her brain as beginning to feel fuzzy.

- Learning can still happen here.

 The Explosion

- Child is yelling.

- Child is screaming.

- Child is hitting.

- Child is kicking.

- Child may throw a fit.

- Child runs away and hides.

- Child calls names.

- Learning is very unlikely at this point.

- Child describes brain as feeling "fuzzy" or "jumbled."

When your child is in the Level Head Stage of Control, things run fairly smoothly. This is the ideal time to have a discussion with your child, if needed, to brainstorm ideas as to how his behavior needs to be adjusted, to discuss discomforting news or topics, or to have a family meeting. Your child will be most agreeable when he's in this stage.

The Ticking Time Bomb Stage of Control is where your child is beginning to show signs that he might be feeling overwhelmed, stressed, frustrated, or angry. This can look a little different for each child, which can make it tricky to identify at first. For some children, their hearts begin to beat faster, their faces may turn red, their expressions may change, or they may become disagreeable.

When a child moves to the Explosion Stage of Control, he's typically crying, yelling, screaming, or arguing without reason. Some children may hit, punch, kick, throw things, or run away from you in these moments as well. Unfortunately, when your child moves to this stage, there isn't a whole lot of learning that can take place. His brain won't even really hear you if you try talking to him during this time. Some children might describe this stage of control as their brain feeling fuzzy or muffled, meaning they're not able to think clearly in these moments. Your job, as his parent, is to make sure your child and those around him are safe. This might mean removing your child from the situation or removing yourself and others, depending on the environment. Even though the child might be running away from you, to know he's safe, you may need to run after him and hold him while he calms down or until you feel he would be ready to calm down on his own.

The Level Head and the Explosion Stages of Control are on opposite ends of a continuum. The most important Stage of Control for you to be aware of and understand as parents is the Ticking Time Bomb Stage. In this stage, you have the opportunity to turn your child's thoughts, feelings, and emotions around. This doesn't mean you give in to your child, but rather you help him find ways to calm down so he can think clearer. Essentially, during this time you want to bring his heart rate back down and to "de-fuzz" his brain. To accomplish this, you need to connect with your child.

Your child might be upset and begin to argue with you because you tell him he needs to clean his room. This type of reaction can be frustrating to get as a parent and often leads to more negative interaction between the parent and child. However, if you know this is the type of situation that often leads to The Explosion (meaning he's in the Ticking Time Bomb Stage when you make this request), it's helpful to place your hand on your child's shoulder or give him a hug from behind as you remind him that this is a simple responsibility that he needs to take care of in the house. For some children, it's the connection through touch that brings their heart rate back down, but for others it's the words.

> **When your child is getting in the Ticking Time Bomb Stage of Control, you need to do two things:**
>
> 1. *Connect with your child.*
>
> 2. *Help bring his heart rate down.*

Eventually, you'll begin to know what types of situations are likely to move your child from the Level Head Stage to the Ticking Time Bomb Stage. For example, some young children tend to get fidgety as the dinner hour approaches. They're tired and hungry, and their coping mechanisms are down. Hence, they're likely to move into the Explosion Stage much quicker than they would at other times during the day. Knowing this, you can prepare ahead of time. Perhaps while you make dinner, your child could play with play dough or paint. This is often a calming activity for young children. Perhaps your parenting partner, if he or she is available to help, could even bathe the child while you make dinner. Bathing is another way to keep the heart rate down and calm your child.

It's important to know that when young children (ages four and under) are starting to move to the Ticking Time Bomb Stage because they're hungry, they might simply need a small, healthy snack while they wait for their dinner (think back to meeting physical needs). As your child gets older, he can begin to learn to cope with these feelings, even if it's feelings of hunger, as long as it's not for long periods of time. If the child consistently moves into the Ticking Time Bomb Stage of Control at the same time each day, it's time to look further at other causes for behavior rather than simply teaching him to cope in the moment. Perhaps your family needs to have dinner at a different time or move bedtimes earlier.

Frustrations in Three-Year-Old Miranda

A couple years ago, Ted and Erika contacted me because they were worried about their three-year-old daughter, Miranda, and her outbursts. They had read about temperament, and they both agreed she was persistent and intense. Over the course of her three years, they had come to really admire these traits in Miranda; however, they didn't want them to come out in such negative ways, as they had been lately. Miranda's brother, Michael, had turned one recently and had become very interested in her toys. This was creating frustration for Miranda.

Ted and Erika also acknowledged that sometimes when Miranda lashed out at Michael or became angry with her parents it was because she was hungry or tired. They had already worked to alleviate these variables, but the issue was still there.

They wanted tools to be able to help Miranda cope with her frustrations. The following shows what these different Stages of Control look like for Miranda from Ted and Erika's perspective.

Example of Miranda's Stages of Control (Age Three)

The Level Head

- Plays happily.
- Smiles at other kids as they approach her at park.
- Talks enthusiastically.
- Is agreeable.
- Enjoys her brother.

The Ticking Time Bomb

- Leaving the park is often difficult. She will begin to whine as her dad starts to gather things to go.
- She tells mom or dad "no."
- She pushes her brother or tells him to move away from her.
- She scrunches her nose and looks extra hard at her point of focus.

The Explosion

- She cries and covers her ears.
- She kicks or hits her brother.
- She runs away from her parents yelling "NO!"
- Her eyes move less and appear to be staring for long periods of time.

It was very helpful for Ted and Erika to identify what these different stages *looked* like. Prior to doing this, it felt that she went from the Level Head to the Explosion in seconds without any warning. However, once they made a list, they discovered some windows of time to divert her emotions. When it was time to let Miranda know that they would be leaving the park, Ted began to come up to tickle her as he told her. He would then play with her the last five minutes to connect and allow her time to explain to him what she had been doing.

Ted and Erika also became more in tune with her playtime with Michael. If they noticed her pushing him away, they would come closer to see if they could offer words for Miranda and Michael to use to negotiate their frustrations. Sometimes they would simply distract Michael so Miranda wouldn't need to be interrupted. Other times, Michael was simply curious about what she was doing, and Ted and Erika wanted her to understand this. In these moments, they would kneel down at her level and explain that Michael was just interested in what she was doing. Then they would ask if she could find a way for Michael to be involved. Words of encouragement were beneficial during these moments as well. Sometimes they would say, "Miranda, your brother admires you so much. He really thinks you're neat. I wonder if we could find a way for him to play *with* you right now."

Outbursts in Eleven-Year-Old Ben

These Stages of Control will look different for every child, not only because of the different temperaments children possess, but also due to age. Shelly and Koren contacted me for insight into their son Ben's outbursts. Ever since Ben was very young, his mood had dictated how the rest of the family felt. When Ben was in a good mood, the family was happy. However, when he was in a foul mood, everyone else's mood altered as well due to the intensity of his emotions. For a long time, Shelly and Koren simply accepted this for what it was. As Ben was getting older, though, they were realizing that he needed to learn some coping skills for his frustrations. I met with Shelly and Koren to go over the Stages of Control and help them identify what these different stages looked like for Ben. The following shows Shelly and Koren's perspective on Ben's Stages of Control.

Example of Ben's Stages of Control (Age Eleven)

The Level Head

- Happy, talkative, smiley, loving.
- Agreeable, conversational.

The Ticking Time Bomb

- Begins to argue.
- Slumps onto couch.
- Says, "I don't know what to do" or "I'm tired."
- Picks on his sister.
- Sighs.
- Grabs at his hair (while doing homework if getting frustrated).

The Explosion

- Calls parents names; sometimes yells, screams.
- Hits his sister.
- Crumples up homework and throws it in garbage.
- Climbs onto couch and cries.
- Brain feels scattered.
- Heart races.

This was a helpful exercise for Ben's parents. The first couple of weeks after Ben's parents were introduced to the Stages of Control thinking, they focused on the specific situations and behaviors they were noticing. A few weeks later, they sat down with Ben to see what his perspective was in regards to these different stages. He was able to add the above descriptions where it says "Brain feels scattered" and "Heart races." They began to discuss with Ben ways he could help calm his heart rate while in the Ticking Time Bomb Stage. He had many ideas, and in fact, they realized that he was already using some of these coping mechanisms at times. For example, sometimes he would simply remove himself from a frustrating situation. When his homework seemed overwhelming, he would walk away and go play basketball across the street at the park for a while. When he returned to his homework, he had a better frame of mind. This was encouraging for his parents, who had been worried about his outbursts. They were glad to know he was developing the capability to calm himself in frustrating situations.

When we have an understanding of our children's behaviors and the Stages of Control, it provides us with insight, which leads to a renewed energy for parenting. Our children, especially those who are five and older, are capable of learning to manage these emotions on their own, or at least with some guidance, when they've been taught these skills and understand them.

Evaluate Further

Before moving on, take time to evaluate how the different Stages of Control look for your child.

1. **What does my child look like in each stage?**
    *   Level Head

    *   Ticking Time Bomb

    *   The Explosion

2. **What situations are likely to bring my child from the Level Head to the Ticking Time Bomb Stage?**

3. **What techniques help my child move from the Ticking Time Bomb to the Level Head Stage?**

CHAPTER FIVE
It's About Learning

Parenting is a hard job. I think most parents know this, but they often don't take enough time to focus on learning the job. When you brought your baby home from the hospital or after adoption, you went through the process of learning about her and she got to know you. Adding subsequent children to your family adds a new element of learning as well. Even when you feel like you might have a handle on this parenting thing, you realize that perhaps you really don't because each child is so different. The reality is that the job of learning about your child and your family is never really complete. Each stage brings new joys and challenges. This can be viewed as daunting or exciting, depending on your perspective. Hopefully, as you're reading this book, you're beginning to use it as a guide that will help your family through these times.

Despite the information you gather through your years as a parent, or even prior to having children, you can never really have all the answers. I've spent years studying child psychology and family development, teaching, working with families, and raising my own children, yet I still feel like there is more for me to learn. I've found it to be incredibly helpful to have a support system to rely on, not only when times get tough, but also when things seem to be going smoothly.

It's the challenging times that seem to stump most parents, though. When you have questions about your child, it's extremely helpful to be able to pick up the phone and call a friend to ask if she has experienced something similar. There are also numerous places you can go to for assistance in understanding your child: the teachers and staff at your child's school, parent consultants, classes for parents, and other professionals, such as social workers and therapists. It's okay to seek out help when it's needed, even if it might seem like a small issue to someone else. If it feels like a big issue to you at the time, it's likely worth looking into to get more information or support for it.

It's important to remember that learning to understand your child is a process.

It's important to remember that learning to understand your child is a process. We live in a society that seeks instant results. Unfortunately, parenting isn't one of those things that you can acquire instant results with. It takes time. Many parents want discipline methods that will be fast. However, many discipline techniques that may create fast results aren't really leading families in the right direction and may actually be counterproductive to the goals parents have for their children.

The Problem with Reward Systems

Before Storm and Jens called me, they had tried a variety of discipline techniques with their six-year-old son, Rocky. When they contacted me, it seemed that Rocky's behavior was improving. Still, they wanted to meet to see if they really were on the right track for their son. They had recently started a behavior chart for Rocky. Every time he did something he wasn't supposed to, he got a frown on his chart and anytime he did something that was "good," he got a smiley face. At the end of dinnertime, they counted the smiley faces and frowns he had acquired throughout the day. On the days he got more smiley faces than frowns, he got to pick out a special dessert to have that night after dinner. Rocky was very excited about this and often checked his chart to see how things were going. He loved having dessert, so this was very motivating to him.

A reward system is a common example of a discipline technique that many parents attempt with their children. They appear to work at first; however, the problem is they don't teach long-term learning. Rocky was starting to control his actions because he wanted to have dessert later. This is helpful in one sense because it tells his parents he's capable of controlling his behavior somewhat; however, this kind of *external motivator* is the *wrong* kind of motivation. It's important to seek out ways for children to be *internally* motivated. In other words, the goal is for Rocky to behave the way that's expected of him because it is the *right thing to do*, it's his responsibility, and he has genuinely learned appropriate behavior.

By giving a reward or praise (saying "Good job" or "That's so wonderful!") to your child, you hope it will make him con-

tinue the action or behavior. Essentially, you're trying to manip-
ulate your child into behaving. In many ways, I think many
parents would agree with this assessment; however, they still
view it as a sound discipline technique. There are many children
who will naturally disregard reward systems. Many children see
through the reward and/or praise. They feel manipulated. They
will think, "Why does she want this so bad for me?" and therefore, power struggles often ensue. I will go into this more in
chapter six.

Alfie Kohn, educator and author, wrote a book, *Punished by
Rewards*, where he shared research on the results and influences of
the use of reward systems and praise. Essentially, he states that
influencing your child with praise or rewards will not teach her
to be intrinsically motivated to choose appropriate behavior. It
may stop the negative behavior briefly and perhaps even altogether, but your child's motivation for discontinuing or continuing, depending on what it is, will not be from within.

Overall, when you're navigating discipline issues, you need
to look at why the behavior might be happening. Ask yourself
the following questions:

- Is it because of my child's developmental level or stage
  (chapter two)?

- What is the goal for or the cause of the behavior
  (chapter three)?

- Is it being accentuated due to my child's temperament
  (chapter four)?

Then, you need to think about how your child will learn to
change the behavior. In other words, how do you teach toward
appropriate behavior so your child internalizes the expected

behavior for the long term? See appendix 3, Behavior Assessment and Action Plan, as a tool you can use with your family to help with this.

Children often learn from trial and error. They also learn by being able to see how their behavior directly affects themselves or others around them. We want the learning to be genuine and influential. We can find things that are influential, such as external rewards, but they usually aren't genuine (real and respectful). As I discussed in chapter three, discipline is the act of giving instruction to another person through patience, understanding, and respect.

Storm and Jens were grateful to have this new insight as they truly wanted Rocky to behave how he should for the right reasons and not just to get ice cream. They decided to talk with Rocky about this concern. They simply told him they didn't want to reward him for his positive behavior any longer. They shared their confidence in him that he was capable of controlling his actions. Rocky said he liked having the smiley faces and frowns, but he agreed he didn't need the ice cream. Storm and Jens decided he could keep the smiley face and frown chart, but he could determine himself if he should place a smiley face or frown on it. Rocky decided he would do this at breakfast, when he got home from school, and after dinner. Soon enough, he moved on from the chart. Rocky and his parents discussed any negative behaviors as they arose, and his actions continued to improve.

Time to Leave the Park

Wendy and Russ were fed up with their three-year-old son's behaviors when they would leave the park. As soon as they told Frankie it was time to go home, he'd run off and play in an area where his parents couldn't reach him. They knew Frankie disliked when they left him at preschool or with a sitter, so it surprised them that he would run away when it was time to go. Wendy and Russ decided to tell him that if he ran away from them at the park again they would leave without him. They knew this would make Frankie nervous, and therefore it would make him come with them when it was time to go.

Wendy and Russ were happy with the results of this experiment. Right when they told Frankie it was time to go, they reminded him that they would leave him there if he didn't come right away. Frankie quickly came over to them to leave together. Wendy and Russ were a little surprised, however, that while he was playing, he came over to them a couple times to make sure they hadn't left him. He often checked in with them, but this time he seemed nervous that they might actually leave. Unfortunately, what Frankie really learned from this was that he needed to worry about whether his parents were going to stick around while he played. Frankie's anxiety regarding being left at preschool and with sitters got worse the next few weeks as Wendy and Russ continued to use this fear-based discipline method. Although this approach certainly had impact and appeared to have worked with Frankie as far as getting him to leave the park without hassle, it was not genuine.

When I first met with Wendy and Russ, they both questioned their current discipline method; however, they were impressed by how well it seemed to work to get Frankie to leave the park. When I explained the idea about long-term learning, they understood why this method wasn't ideal. I helped Wendy and Russ create a new plan for situations they were encountering when leaving the park that was both influential and genuine.

First, I recommended they sit down with Frankie prior to their next park visit to discuss the issue. Wendy and Russ needed to explain that if they were going to continue visiting the park, their family needed a new plan for when it was time to leave. I will go into further detail in chapter nine on family meetings and discussions. Wendy and Russ told Frankie that they would be sure to give him a five-minute warning before it would be time to leave the park. At that time, Frankie was to choose one more thing to do: one more time down the slide, one more climb up the ladder, et cetera. The family was then to meet at the pavilion for a quick drink of water before leaving together. The situation will predictably get better for two reasons: 1) Frankie would feel respected, since Wendy and Russ were genuine with him by involving him in the discussion about how to address this issue and 2) their family created a plan for when it was time to leave the park. Frankie's behavior at the park was likely related to power. By including him in the discussion, he felt he had power in the situation and knew what was expected.

Frankie is not perfect, however, so occasionally he forgets or chooses differently than he knows he should. In these cases, rather than using the previous scare tactic with him, Wendy and Russ had a backup plan in place. If Frankie chose to run and hide when it was time to go, his parents immediately caught him (yes, they sometimes needed to run to do this). Once he was caught, they didn't laugh, even though Frankie may have laughed at this time. There was also no need to yell. Simply catching Frankie, carrying him to the car, and saying, "We must go home now. Perhaps next time you'll make a different choice" was influential enough. If it happened a second time, then a break from the park helped send the message to Frankie that his behavior wasn't okay. When Wendy and Russ told Frankie he needed a break from the park, they needed to follow through on this. Actions speak louder than words. These lessons may take a while to learn, but be confident knowing that learning is happening, even if it may be slow.

Time Outs

Time outs are another popular discipline technique and are commonly recommended in parenting classes, parenting books, and parenting magazines. Most parents hope that during a time out, the child will think about his actions and make better choices after resuming play. However, most children spend the time feeling mad and upset and don't think about what they should learn from the situation. Time outs can also feel shameful to children because they diminish their self-respect and their respect for the person who punished them. Hence, the typical use of time outs is ineffective in teaching children to internalize the expected behaviors and actions.

The typical use of time outs is ineffective in teaching children to internalize the expected behaviors and actions.

There are a variety of ways to approach behavioral concerns

or issues, and many of these we've discussed in previous chapters. Sometimes your child will certainly need a break from playing. If your child is out of control, he certainly shouldn't be allowed to continue that behavior. Instead of placing him in a time out, he may need assistance calming down so you can get to the root of the issue. Many times, children are simply tired and need some downtime when behavioral issues arise. Maybe a break to take a nap or rest is needed. Often parents allow their child to watch TV or a video during downtime. However, many times, with the bright lights and action, watching TV doesn't count as true downtime, especially for young children.

When my son was young, books were always calming to him. When he would lose control or begin to feel frustrated with himself or others, I would either read a book with him or bring him over to a basket of books for him to look at so he could regroup. The idea was for him to bring his heart rate down. Sometimes he needed assistance with this, and other times he was capable of doing it on his own as he looked through books. There wasn't a set time he needed to stay there. He didn't resist this because of the words I used. I would say, "I can tell your body needs to calm down. You can look at some books for a couple minutes to calm yourself. When your body feels quiet, you're welcome to come join us again." When I wondered if he might resist, I would simply sit with him. I wanted my son to begin to understand what his body needed when he was beginning to lose control or had lost control. It needed to be calmed down. For him, looking at books helped. For another child, it might be something else: listening to music, snuggling with a certain toy, or playing with play dough.

I've been criticized on this technique before. Many people

wonder if it's actually rewarding the child for negative behavior. When looking at the root of the challenging behavior, it's important to remember that most of the time the behavior is stemming from something else other than the moment at hand. If your child is getting frustrated with his sibling and eventually takes a swing at her, you'll want to pull the child aside. If you put your hand on your child's chest at the time, his heart rate will likely be raised. As I discussed in the last chapter, when a child has a raised heart rate, he can't think as clearly. Before you spend time trying to teach the lesson from the moment, you'll want to find a way for the child's heart rate to come down. Once the heart rate comes down, he will likely be able to choose different behavior because his needs of calming down will have been met. This method provides a respectful way for your child to regroup and is much like when my family pulled over when we were lost in California. Once we had a chance to regroup, we were able to face the challenge ahead of us.

There are, however, moments where *you*, as the parent, might need a time out. Believe me, I've been there. In these moments, it's important to step away, even if it's only for a couple seconds. If you find you're having more days than not that you're feeling this way, then it's important to make a new plan. There's no such thing as a perfect parent. You will make mistakes; everyone does. Like you hope to do with your child, you need to be patient with yourself. When you find yourself getting frustrated, take deep breaths, walk away briefly, like I mentioned above, and try to focus on the positive traits your child possesses. It can be easy to focus on the negative behaviors, forgetting all the positive interactions that happen at other times. Perhaps it's appropriate to look into resources that could be helpful to you: a babysitter for a couple hours every few days, some help with cooking or cleaning, some input from a parent consultant or therapist, or some scheduled play times with other parents and their children. Staying calm certainly isn't always easy. If you keep your compass close by, you'll be back on your way again soon enough.

Evaluate Further

As the final chapter in this section comes to a close, take some time to think about the following questions:

1. How do I feel/react when I'm yelled at or made to feel ashamed of the mistakes I've made?

2. How do I feel/react when someone is patient with me when I've made a mistake?

3. Thinking about the above questions, which person would I feel more connected to and want to listen to in the future: the person who yelled at me and made me feel ashamed or the person who was patient with me?

SECTION THREE

Independence

Throughout this section of the book, you'll learn about the importance of inde-pendence in your child's life, even from a very young age.

- *Chapter six discusses how independence in children has changed over the course of the past twenty to thirty years and how this is influencing children in negative ways. I'll walk you through how you can find ways for your child to have some independence in his life, no matter what his current age.*

- *In chapter seven, you'll look at how independence influences disci-pline. I'll introduce you to a tool that can be used to help your child see his responsibilities as truly his, rather than things he simply is told he needs to do.*

Independence is a key factor in guiding your child through the years of his life. Without knowledge of this important aspect, your family won't have a well-working compass for the journey. Your child will be misguided and will need to rely on you into adulthood more than is appropriate.

CHAPTER SIX
The Key to Empowerment

I remember numerous days throughout my childhood when I'd head out with my friends to explore the outskirts of our neighborhood: riding bikes back and forth between our friends' houses, exploring in the surrounding woods, and biking to town. Sometimes we encountered obstacles: the ferocious dog, a flat tire (and no cell phones then!), or a skinned knee with no adult around to help bandage it up. Although some of those moments felt scary, we always managed to figure out a way to cope. Our tree-climbing skills quickly increased as we learned to get away from the dog. We learned that it's not all bad to have to walk a bike back home from town with a flat tire, although it did take more time. We eventually figured out that perhaps we should carry a quarter to make a phone call at the gas station if we needed to reach our parents. We also learned that wiping our skinned knee with the inside of our shirt worked just fine until we could get to a better place to clean it.

We'd go home at the end of those days feeling proud of our explorations and feats that we accomplished along the way. As long as we arrived at home at the time specified, we were allowed to head back out on the next adventure the following day. Now that was powerful!

There was little need to argue with our parents or disagree about doing chores around the house on those nights. We felt emotionally fulfilled because we had gained a new sense of independence and confidence on each of these adventures. We also felt respected by our parents that *they* felt confident in our abilities to be independent throughout the day. Rarely do children in today's American culture have such experiences.

What Shifted?

Life has changed. Parents in today's culture are often ridiculed by other parents for allowing their children the types of freedoms I experienced as a child. In 2008, Lenore Skenazy wrote an article in New York's *The Sun* about why she allowed her nine-year-old son to ride the subway and bus all by himself: to provide him with the independence she knew he was ready for. Soon enough she was labeled America's worst mom through the media. She was even asked to be a guest on *The Today Show* to defend why she felt this was an appropriate independent activity for her child.

Whether or not you agree with Skenazy's decision is irrelevant here. The important thing to consider is that society's strong reaction to this mother's choice comes from fear. Parents fear for the safety of their children. These fears started growing in the 1980s and have continued to increase. The media have provided society with great information about child abductions and child predators. News outlets also brought these situations into living rooms across America. So, unfortunately, parents feel the likelihood of this happening to their child or in their neighborhood is very high.

In 1989, I was thirteen years old when a Minnesota boy, Jacob Wetterling, was kidnapped at gunpoint while out on an evening bike ride with his brother and friend. Jacob was twelve years old. This hit home to me. If this could happen to a twelve-year-old kid in Minnesota, it could happen to me. Although the town Jacob lived in was more than an hour away from my town, it still changed my neighborhood. Younger children were suddenly not playing outside anymore unless their parents were with them or they were right in their own yard. My neighbor friend suddenly had to walk her six-year-old sister to her friend's house that was only four houses away. Because of traumatic events, such as child abductions, parents hover over their children, don't let them out of their sight, and don't provide them with freedoms they're likely ready for.

Because of traumatic events, such as child abductions, parents hover over their children, don't let them out of their sight, and don't provide them with freedoms they're likely ready for.

These fears have led to a rise in organized activities for children, as parents don't want their children out alone. When children are involved in an organized activity, parents know where they are. It eases their minds. The business of organized children's activities has taken off over the years. Many organizations now offer daily activities for children as young as one and a half years old. Parents see these activities offered and think, "My child must need this," even if it's a gymnastics class for a two-year-old. Children spend more time involved in organized activities each day than they do in free-play activities (Elkind, 2008).

Countless children have very full schedules: soccer practices, piano lessons, choir, and karate are examples. There's nothing wrong with all of these activities; however, they often fill so much of a child's schedule that she doesn't have time to simply play or take part in household responsibilities. Parents see that the child is busy, so they don't ask her to take on any tasks around the house.

When two-parent working families and single-parent families are added to this mix, we're faced with extremely busy households. When parents are busy, they're more likely to do things for their child that she's more than capable of doing for herself, such as tying her shoes, folding her laundry, and cleaning her room. Even more so, parents don't feel they have the time to teach their child tasks that she may be ready to learn. This is a concern, not only for the development of the child, but for the development of society. Today's children will grow to be adults. If they haven't been taught how to care for themselves efficiently (leading to helplessness) and how to think beyond themselves (leading to a continuation of egocentricity), they won't flourish in the adult role.

Why Is the Lack of Independence Harmful to Children?

Many children are entering kindergarten not knowing how to zip their own coats, pull their snow pants over their boots, and wipe their own noses. Numerous middle school students don't know how to scramble eggs, clean a toilet, or wash dishes. Countless teens don't know how to do their own laundry until they leave for college and are forced to do it themselves. In this day and age, many parents of postcollege students are joining their children for job interviews or mailing resumes on their child's behalf. A Michigan State University survey of 725 employers in 2007 discovered that nearly one third (31 percent) had seen a parent submit a resume for their child. Most of the time, the motivation behind helping children with these tasks comes out of a deep love for them. Parents want their child to be successful. But, the truth is, parents are taking away some of their child's true potential for success when they don't allow him to learn these necessary tasks and responsibilities.

When parents control and manage their children's lives too much, the children are at a disadvantage.

It's important for children to have recurring experiences where they're allowed independence. When parents control and manage their children's lives too much, the children are at a disadvantage. Dr. David Bredehoft, professor of psychology at Concordia University in St. Paul, Minnesota, has done numerous research studies on overindulgence: what happens when someone is allowed too much or too little of something, such as too much attention, too little discipline, or not enough independence. He shares this research in a book he wrote in 2009 with Jean Illsley Clarke and Connie Dawson, titled *How Much Is Enough?* He interviewed adults who were overindulged as children in three different areas:

- **Too Much:** given too many things
- **Soft Structure:** given too much freedom
- **Over-nurturing:** given too much care and attention

Dr. Bredehoft measured how the adults in the study were influenced when they were overindulged as children. Over-nurturing had the most significant effect on one's ability to become independent, since the parent had done so much for the child. The adults in the studies reported that they felt frustrated with their parents that they didn't know how to do many of the skills that other adults knew how to do because their parents did these things for them. They felt helpless.

Sometimes your child will show you signs that your current parenting practices aren't working for him: he will begin to push back, engage in power struggles, or act helpless. Even if your child isn't showing these signs, it's important for you to assess if you might be over-nurturing him.

What Can We Do?

Today's American society will only allow children to be somewhat independent. This makes more work for parents to create means for independence at home and through family life. This can begin at very young ages. The problem is you need to make sure your child is experiencing the *right* kind of independence so she isn't seeking out the *wrong* kind. When children feel a sense of independence and confidence, they're less likely to push back when a request is made of them.

In his 2009 book, *Drive*, Daniel Pink discusses how it's feelings of autonomy (independence) that motivate people. Without autonomy, people can feel stifled and unsure of their direction. Children feel this as well, yet they would rarely be able to articulate this. A child who's simply told what to do all the time may fall in line and do as he's told and may appear to be unaf-

When people, children included, are provided with autonomous experiences, they thrive.

fected. However, he'll likely seem unexcited and uninspired to try new things. Eventually, he may lose the desire to even think for himself.

When people, children included, are provided with autonomous experiences (see appendix 1 for examples for children), they thrive. They feel intrinsically motivated, gain confidence quickly, and want to be the best they can be. People, including children, "are not destined to be passive and compliant" (Pink, 2009). Rather, they are destined to be actively involved in their thinking and learning, which creates feelings of power and control.

Think about the young toddler who's allowed to walk alongside his stroller rather than be buckled inside. He'll naturally feel confident and powerful as he's experimenting with his newfound walking skills. He may even enjoy pushing the stroller as he sees it's something *you* usually get to do. In most situations, this will be a fine activity for your child to do with supervision.

Your toddler will be less likely to engage you in a power struggle later in the day when a necessary request is made of him because he'll be emotionally fulfilled from these opportunities to feel big and powerful.

Independence at Its Best

In the summer, I run a program that's located on a six-ty-acre farm in Minnesota attended by children ages two-and-a-half to ten years old. As part of the curriculum, the children take part in all aspects of the farm: planting seeds, tending to the garden, feeding and bringing water to the animals, and other animal care. I often hear from parents that the children love the program because of the animals. Although this is a wonderful aspect of the school, and one that sets it apart from other sum-mer enrichment opportunities, the animals aren't the real reason why children want to come back summer after summer. The secret is that they want to come back because of how they *feel* when they're there. They love coming to the farm because . . .

- Someone thinks enough of them to ask them to carry water over to the sheep.

- They get to see that they're strong enough to carry a bale of hay, even if it's only for a couple feet.

- They pull weeds from their garden and get to see that their plants grow better without the weeds surround-ing them.

- They enjoy helping other children move the goats out of the pen so everyone can pet them easier when they're tied out on ropes.

Participating in these types of activities is very empowering to children. It's these feelings of the *right* kind of power (independence) that lead to genuine feelings of happiness and confidence.

Many years ago, there was a four-year-old child, Havana, in one of my summer classes at the farm. Havana's mother had contacted me before she started that summer. She told me that Havana was a very difficult child who was constantly arguing, negotiating, and throwing tantrums at home. As a teacher, it can be helpful to have this information prior to working with a child. However, I also know that children can act very different depending on the environment. I listened to the information Havana's mom shared with me, but I also went into my time with her with an open mind.

From the first day of class, it was obvious that Havana enjoyed the reward of caring for the animals. She smiled as she fed them and talked about how they needed her so they wouldn't go hungry. She especially enjoyed pushing the wheelbarrows full of hay to the goats and carrying buckets of water to be dumped in the large horse trough. She was thriving in our program.

Havana's time at the farm continued to be successful. On the last day of the class, her mom came up to me and gave me a big hug. She went on to tell me how her daughter was a changed child since she started in our program. She told me that Havana no longer challenged her on every little thing and was now actually very cooperative. She wondered what I did to change her daughter. It was simple, really. In our program, Havana was provided numerous opportunities to be independent, which led to feelings of the *right* kind of power, so she no longer felt the need to seek out the *wrong* kind of power at home.

Choices

We often hear that children need choices. They need choices because they need to feel in control of their life. I agree with this; however, it's often misinterpreted. Children are often given the *wrong* kind of power and control rather than the *right* kind as I mentioned above. Dr. Bredehoft found this to be true in his research as well. He referred to this as *Soft Structure*, where the children were given too many choices for their age and developmental level. This often leads to the child having more power in the household than the parents, resulting in a child who isn't genuinely happy and confident.

Last year, I was contacted by a mom, Stacy, whom I had met the year prior at a workshop I had led. She contacted me because her eight-year-old daughter, Gabby, was beginning to have problems in school. Her teacher said she was manipulating her friends during activities so she could always be the one in charge. Gabby is an only child and has always enjoyed being a leader. Stacy really likes this about Gabby, but she had noticed that it was feeling more like manipulation than leadership.

When Gabby was three, her mom played dress up with her. Gabby got to choose exactly what her mom would wear and how she would wear it. If Gabby wanted to add something from her mom's closet to her own ensemble, she was usually allowed to do it, including her mom's antique diamond necklace. When Gabby played with her friends, she led the play in the same way.

Since Gabby was very young, Stacy made sure that Gabby knew ahead of time what would be for dinner at night. If Gabby decided she would like an alternative meal, her mom would make her a separate dish. Sometimes, Gabby changed her mind at the last minute, even after an additional meal had been made for her. Stacy felt like this was a good option for Gabby, as it provided her with a choice and control over what she was eating. Yet it did bother Stacy if Gabby changed her mind. Still, Stacy is a picky eater, too, so she felt like this was a respectful way to approach Gabby's pickiness. She wished her parents would have taken this approach with her as a child; however, she acknowledges that she would likely be even pickier now as an adult if her parents would have simply fed her what she liked.

Gabby also never liked going to bed at night. Stacy decided a couple years ago that perhaps by allowing her to choose her own bedtime she would start to enjoy this time of night more. Rarely did Gabby choose to go to bed before 9 p.m., even on school nights. Stacy encouraged her to go to sleep sooner, but she felt like Gabby could handle this choice. When Gabby did decide it was time to go to bed, she got to decide where she would sleep that night: her bed, her mom's bed, or on the couch.

Gabby is a child who's been given a great deal of choices. Her mom knew that choices were important to children as they aid in feelings of power. However, the type of choices that Gabby was provided were examples of the *wrong* kind of power. Stacy meant well and had taken time to think through her decisions, but the results unfortunately had given Gabby a false sense of power. Gabby assumed everyone else would give her this kind of control and actually started to think she deserved more power than anyone else.

In the first chapter, I shared the importance of setting family goals. When Stacy took the time to examine her long-term goals for Gabby, she realized that she wasn't always parenting toward these goals. She had been encouraging Gabby's independence, which was a characteristic she wanted to foster. However, she had been neglecting to focus on some of the other values she had for her daughter: learning respect for others, along with having the ability to think beyond herself.

Let's start by looking back at Gabby as a three-year-old playing dress up with her mom. Children love to lead play, and when adults play with children, it's appropriate to allow them to lead a portion of it, rather than take it over. When an adult plays with a child, it's preparation for playing with her peers later. If the adult allows the child to make all the decisions in the play, the child is learning that this is how it will go when she plays with her peers as well. Instead of allowing Gabby to tell her mom what to wear for dress up, her mom could have said, "That would look nice, but I really want to wear this outfit instead." Even if the adult isn't feeling manipulated by the child at the time, it's important to think through what the child might be learning through that play.

There are many households that handle dinner in the same manner that Stacy had been choosing to handle it with Gabby. You want to respect your child, but what ends up happening is that you can lose your own self-respect by becoming a short-order cook. Giving Gabby the power to choose what she would be served for dinner each night was giving her *too much* power. This is an example of the *wrong* kind of power. Stacy was very surprised by this and previously felt like this was one of the things that made her such a caring mom—the fact that she respected her daughter enough to not serve her food she didn't like. You can't force your child to eat, and I would never recommend you do. However, I can tell you that when children are served a variety of foods that are also being offered to the rest of their family, they will eventually grow in their comfort and likes of food. This won't change instantly, of course, and if your family is going to make this change, there will initially be resistance.

When introducing a change like this to children (ages three years and older), I recommend you do it in the context of a family meeting, which I will discuss further in chapter nine. If your children are younger than three years old, you can gradually make this change without addressing it with them first. Be sure to always offer one food you know she'll like as you're introducing new foods. It's important to eliminate snacking on crackers and drinking juice and other beverages that are more of a supplement as you're making this change. This will eliminate the possibility of your child getting full on these items and not being open to trying the other foods.

If your child is age three or older, she can assist you with coming up with family meals for the week. She can also help with cooking these meals and setting the table. It's beneficial to offer the food family style so your child can choose how much food to take. These are all examples of the *right* kind of power. If your child doesn't eat what's served to her, she can pack it up (if she's old enough to do this) and can have it later when she says she's hungry or can simply wait until the next snack or meal would typically be served. If your child is underweight or there are medical issues, please consult with your child's physician prior to making this type of change in the foods served to her.

Bedtime issues are challenging in many homes. However,

giving a child Gabby's age control of her bedtime isn't appropriate. You can't force your child to sleep, but you can provide a consistent bedtime routine and a set time that the lights need to be out. This will promote security in your child. If there are control issues surrounding bedtime, perhaps it's time for your family to have a discussion to make a new plan. Again, I will go into more detail about family discussions in chapter nine. Perhaps Gabby could decide which book she will read before bed or if she would rather shower or take a bath during her bedtime routine. Stacy could help her rearrange her room in a way that appeals to her so she will be more inclined to sleep in there. These are all examples of the *right* kind of power for a child this age.

Stacy was very responsive to the feedback I provided to her about Gabby and power. I explained to her that the issues Gabby was having at school wouldn't get better instantly. Gabby needed to be retaught some things. Stacy set up a meeting with Gabby's teacher to explain what she would be working on with Gabby at home and offer her support for how it would be addressed at school. Some of the issues would create natural consequences. For example, if Gabby wasn't provided with more opportunities for the *right* kind of power and continued to have the *wrong* kind of power, her friends may very likely decide her friendship isn't worth having.

I checked in with Stacy recently and she said that things have improved with Gabby dramatically. Initially, though, it was challenging for Stacy to stick with her new plan. She felt guilty that she was taking some control away from Gabby, even though she understood it was the wrong kind of control for a child her age. Gabby was resistant to new foods at first, but she gradually has become more open-minded. Stacy no longer feels manipulated and has more time to enjoy the meals with her daughter than she did before. Gabby's still struggling socially at times, but the teachers and Stacy are continuing to guide her through this.

How Do I Know if It's the *Right* Kind or the *Wrong* Kind of Power?

When trying to decipher between what might be considered the *right* kind of power and the *wrong* kind of power, you'll want to think about the message that's being sent to your child and how it would be interpreted by others. If you answer "yes" to the following questions, your child is likely being allowed the *wrong* kind of power:

- Do I feel manipulated by my child?
- Even if *I* don't feel manipulated by my child, might someone else in that situation?
- If my child was in this situation with a friend, would this other child feel overpowered?
- Is my child struggling with the power I've given her?

Sometimes something is the *wrong* kind of power because of your child's age and maturity. For example, your eight-year-old shouldn't be allowed to choose her own bedtime; however, your young teenager should be able to make this decision with some guidance. If your teen is struggling with this decision, then it would be time to provide her with more guidance in this area. See table 4 for some general examples of these two different kinds of power.

TABLE 4

Distinguishing Between the Right and Wrong Kind of Power for Children

Examples of the Right Kind of Power	Examples of the Wrong Kind of Power
Child helps around the house and yard.	Child decides if he's going to attend the summer camp he is signed up for.
Child cares for pets and other living things.	Child decides on own bedtime (prior to early to midteen years and he will still need guidance from parents on this).
Child helps make decisions about bedtime routine (once child is five and older).	Child is allowed to change rules of the game without the other players' consent and desire.
Child is allowed to walk rather than being contained in stroller or parent's arms.	Child is allowed to negotiate out of chores or other family expectations.
Provide the child with time to prepare for schedule change or transition by saying, "It's going to be time to leave in five more minutes. This is enough time for you to go down the slide five more times or you can ride around the park one time on your bike. When you've done one of those, it's time to go."	Child allowed to dictate if the family is going to go somewhere (unless this is set up ahead of time and is a rarity rather than the norm).

Examples of the Right Kind of Power	Examples of the Wrong Kind of Power
Child can help be a part of meal planning for the family.	Child is allowed to tell parent no or is generally allowed to talk back to parents in a negative way.
Child has independence with play and does not need to be entertained.	Child tells parent what to do.
Child does service work with family, friends, school, or church.	
Child is involved in family discussions.	
Child wears a watch so he can take responsibility for when he needs to be home (depending on the neighborhood and maturity of child, of course, but could begin around kindergarten).	

How Independence Affects Children in Positive Ways: One Family's Story

Last year I worked with the Sanchez family. They have one son, Luis, who was two-and-a-half years old at the time. Luis was pretty laid back when he was with his dad, Manuel. However, when he was with his mom, Nina, she said he was whiny and rarely tried to do things on his own. Nina started to wonder why he was like this and noticed that other kids his age didn't act the same way. When I sat down to talk with Manuel and Nina, Luis was alongside us for a while before his babysitter came to play with him in another room. During the time while I was getting to know the Sanchez family, I observed how their interactions influenced Luis.

Manuel offered Luis a snack. He did this by asking Luis to come over to the pantry to pick out one type of cracker. Then they counted out six crackers for him to eat. Luis carried his bowl over to the table, but before he could sit down, Nina picked him up and put him on her lap. At first, he tried to squirm away, but then he settled in. I tried talking to Luis, but he suddenly hid his face in his mom's sleeve. Prior to this, he had been smiling at me and even showed me some of his toys by reaching them out to me. Nina looked at me and said, "He's really shy." Manuel asked Nina to put him down, which she did, and Luis walked over to his seat to sit down. He then smiled at me again and handed me a cracker.

We were sharing in small talk as Luis finished his snack. When he was done, he hopped off his chair. His dad reminded him to carry his bowl to the counter, but Nina said, "I can get it for you, honey." She then picked him up and carried him as she placed his bowl on the counter. I could tell Nina enjoyed her son very much, but I wondered how Luis was perceiving her interactions with him.

When Nina put Luis down again, he went over to a puzzle that he had been playing with when I arrived. Just minutes before, he didn't have any trouble with this puzzle. He would look at the pieces, experiment, and find a place for them. However, this time he turned to his mom and said, "Help me, Mommy. I can't do it." Nina looked at me as if to say, "This is what I mean." She then sat down to help him.

After Luis's babysitter arrived, I shared my observations with his parents. I first asked them if the interactions were typical. They said yes, and Nina even asked if I noticed how much needier Luis was with her than with Manuel. I told her I did notice this. Manuel spoke up right away and said, "I think he acts this way because you treat him like he should act this way." Nina looked stunned, and she asked him to clarify. He went on to explain that he noticed that as soon as she picked Luis up he acted younger. "He acts like you think he can't do some of these bigger things," Manuel said. Nina defended herself by saying she loves this time with Luis and that she likes that he's still small enough for her to pick him up. She said she wants him to know how much she loves him. Manuel looked hurt. "Do you think he doesn't think *I* love him?" he said.

Some parents think they show love to their children by giving them what they want and holding them. However, there are many ways you can tell your child you love him. Interacting with him in a way that shows you have confidence in him is the best way to do this. Can you still hug your child and pick him up every once in a while for some holding? Absolutely! However, if this happens more often than not, the message that's actually being sent to him is that he's small and that he needs you to protect him all the time. Unfortunately, that message isn't very empowering.

Manuel, Nina, and I continued to talk about these interactions for quite a while. Nina acknowledged that this wasn't going to be easy for her to make these changes, but she saw the importance. I equipped Nina with some words of encouragement that she could use with Luis (see appendix 4 for examples). We also discussed the zone of proximal development (ZPD) and how she could use this theory to help her stretch Luis to where he's ready to be developmentally.

I continued to stay in touch with Nina over the course of the next month. She wanted to meet for a quick follow-up to discuss how things had been going. She was thrilled to share some of Luis's accomplishments. She said her son was like a new kid: very confident and asking for even more independence now. As I was leaving that day, Nina gave me a big hug and said, "I never would have thought we could bring happiness to our child in such a simple way. We would do anything as parents to help him be happy. We'd give him attention, toys, ANYTHING! Now we see that independence is really the thing that makes him happy. Thank you!"

"I never would have thought we could bring happiness to our child in such a simple way.

We would do anything as parents to help him be happy. We'd give him attention, toys, ANYTHING! Now we see that independence is really the thing that makes him happy."

As long as independence is provided with love and confidence, she's right—it's that easy!

Evaluate Further

As you finish this chapter on the importance of independence for your child through this journey, take time to think about the following questions:

I. In what ways does my child have independence at home right now? Mark which of these would fall under the *right* kind or the *wrong* kind of power.

2. What are three things I can do to foster more independence in my child that are the *right* kind of power?

3. What other adults do I need on board for this?

CHAPTER SEVEN
Impact of Independence on Discipline

When your child feels a sense of the *right* kind of power and control (independence), she's going to have more buy-in when it comes to discipline. In chapter five, I discussed the downside of using rewards and praise to increase positive behavior in your child. Again, many children, especially those who are very perceptive, will likely pick up on the fact that they're being manipulated. This, more often than not, leads to power struggles.

Another discipline method that's often used is taking away items from a child when she doesn't do what's expected of her. When you put yourself in a position of providing a reward or punishment to your child for her behavior, you have more control than you should have. You're supposed to help guide your child by teaching her right and wrong. However, if you choose to go about this through rewards and praise and/or inflicting punishment on your child, she'll feel like it's being done *to* her. When something feels like it's being done *to* her, she'll naturally feel like she has less control and it will promote less buy-in than if it was presented to her differently. As I stated in chapter five, you want your child to do what's right because it's the right thing to do and not because she might lose or gain something for doing it or not doing it.

You might tell your child that if he doesn't clean up his room he can't play with his friends later. This makes sense; however, you have to be careful with how it's presented. If it feels like you're taking this away from him, he'll simply be mad and less likely to clean his room in the end. Or, he will clean it, but he won't be learning the true meaning behind responsibility. However, if he feels like this is a choice he's making, he's more likely to complete the necessary task and take responsibility for the fact that it's *his* task to complete. You can say, "When you've cleaned your room, you can play with your friends." If the child says he's not cleaning his room, you can respond by saying, "I know you were excited to play with Joe and Jack today. It's your choice, but if you want to play with your friends, you'll need to clean your room first."

You want to set up discipline in a way that your child feels as though he's a part of it. Your child needs to know that he can be in control of the choices he makes for himself and that these choices influence others and himself. Many times when a child is resistant to chores or other expectations, it's because he thinks he has a right to do what he wants and that these chores or tasks are the responsibility of someone else. Most children don't yet understand the differences between rights and privileges and needs and wants. Furthermore, many children don't fully grasp what their responsibilities are and how these responsibilities affect their involvement in other activities. You need to help your child create these categories in his mind: needs, responsibilities, rights, and privileges.

I developed a tool (Needs to Privileges) for you to use to teach your child to think in these terms. This should be done in the context of a family meeting (see chapter nine) and can be used with children roughly age six and older. First, you'll share the four categories with your child—Needs, Responsibilities, Rights, and Privileges—along with the definitions for each. Then, as a family, begin to fill in items in the different categories. The main idea is to help your child see that you all have responsibilities in life and that before you can enjoy privileges (the extras in life) you need to take care of these responsibilities. Many children see their privileges as their rights rather than as extras that are above and beyond what's really needed.

Needs to Privileges

Needs
Definition: A requirement to function properly
  Examples from one family:
  • School/Education

  • Bathing

  • Food

  • Shelter

Responsibilities

Definition: Something that needs to be taken care of, that we need to be responsible for

Examples from one family:

- Cleaning the house
- Preparing meals
- Shoveling snow
- Taking care of pets
- Making money to pay the bills
- Doing laundry
- Cleaning up after self
- Getting homework done

Rights

Definition: Something that we are allowed

Examples from one family:

- Alone time
- Exercise
- Clean sheets on beds
- Respectful interactions

Privileges or Extras

Definition: A special opportunity

Examples from one family:

- Being on sports teams
- Going to sporting events
- TV/Computer time/Video games

- New clothes
- To buy things
- Going to friends' houses/having friends over

Using these terms, definitions, and examples will help make your child feel more involved in his own discipline and gives him ownership. It helps him make the connection that responsibilities need to be met before privileges are allowed and that your job, as his parent, is to make sure his needs are met and everybody's rights are respected. This puts the accountability on your child, rather than on you.

For your child to become independent and self-disciplined, you need to guide him through this process of understanding what his role is in his own life.

You won't need to take something away from your child for not doing what's expected of him because he made the choice not to complete his responsibilities. It isn't a right to go to hockey practice, but rather a privilege. This means that if homework (responsibility) isn't done before hockey practice (a privilege) and it was supposed to be, then hockey practice can't happen on this day. There's no need for you to pass this message along to your child in an angry tone, but rather in a matter-of-fact tone. It's not your child's punishment (remember the distinction made between discipline and punishment in chapter three), but rather the way for him to see the effect of his choices. As soon as you add anger or shame into the mix, your child quickly feels like this is being done *to* him, which provokes a powerless feeling. For your child to become independent and self-disciplined, you need to guide him through this process of understanding what his role is in his own life.

Needs to Privileges: One Family's Story

As the Carolle family finished up dinner, Jed and Leslie looked at each other, took a deep breath, and whispered, "You ready for this?" They knew they needed to prepare themselves for the battles that had been ensuing between dinnertime and bedtime each night with their three children, ages thirteen, eleven, and nine. It should be simple, they thought: dinner needed to get cleaned up, homework needed to get done, showers needed to be taken, and all three kids needed to be in bed by 9:15 p.m. However, it hadn't been very simple lately. Over the past couple weeks, they had been attempting to give the children more responsibility around the house. It was currently backfiring.

As Brandon, the eleven-year-old, stood up, he said, "It's not my turn to help clean up. I'm out of here!" He leapt off of his chair and ran downstairs. Was he off to do his homework? Likely not. Molly, age thirteen, got up and looked at her parents and then at her sister and said, "I'm not doing it either. Guess it's your turn tonight, Peyton!" She then left the kitchen. Jed immediately got up and hollered to Brandon to come upstairs to start his homework. Brandon yelled that he was in the middle of something, so he couldn't come up yet. By this time, Molly had disappeared too. Leslie looked at Peyton and said, "Guess it's you and me tonight." Peyton's shoulders dropped and she said, "Why do I always have to help? I have to do everything around here!" This of course was not true.

Eventually Jed found Molly, who by this time was on the phone with one of her friends. Jed signaled for her to finish up and she pushed her door shut so she couldn't hear him anymore. This, of course, made Jed angry. So he opened the door back up. Molly hung up the phone and said, "You need to knock when you come in my room, Dad!" He agreed with this normally, but she didn't shut the door until he was right there and she knew very well that she was avoiding her responsibilities at the time. This was out of hand, he thought to himself.

For many years, Jed and Leslie weren't sure what household responsibilities they should expect of their children. Lately, they noticed the children weren't showing much appreciation for the things their parents did for them. They were becoming demanding and disrespectful to their parents. Jed and Leslie knew they needed a change. However, their attempt to make these changes was not going well. The children didn't understand why they suddenly had to help more, and Jed and Leslie weren't sure how to present it to the children so it would have a positive and long-term effect on their family.

I met with the Carolle family to introduce the Needs-to-Privileges tool to them to help get their kids on track for helping around the house and for the kids to learn a sense of appreciation. The Carolles went over this together as a family. The children began to see that everyone in the family should have responsibilities. They decided to revisit this chart often to add to it. The parents finally felt like they had a way to talk to their children about these issues. They made it very clear that the children were in charge of their responsibilities and that if those basic responsibilities weren't taken care of, the extras couldn't happen. The children had control of this. Their evening struggles gradually began to fade and their children began to show more respect toward their parents and each other. Table 5 shows the results of the Carolles' discussion.

TABLE 5

The Carolle Family Needs-to-Privileges

Needs				
Jed	Leslie	Molly	Brandon	Peyton
Sleep	Sleep	Sleep	Sleep	Sleep
Food	Food	Food	Food	Food
Shelter	Shelter	Shelter	Shelter	Shelter
Bathing	Bathing	School/ Education	School/ Education	School/ Education
Clothes	Clothes	Bathing	Bathing	Bathing
		Clothes	Clothes	Clothes

Responsibilities				
Jed	Leslie	Molly	Brandon	Peyton
Work to make money for the family.	Work part time to help supplement income for family.	Go to school and get homework done.	Go to school and get homework done.	Go to school and get homework done.
Manage finances for the family.	Cook the family meals.	Keep room presentable.	Keep room presentable.	Keep room presentable.
Maintain family vehicles.	Organize the cleaning for the house.	Help clean up dinner a couple times per week.	Clean up game room two times per week.	Help clean up dinner a couple times per week.

Responsibilities				
Jed	Leslie	Molly	Brandon	Peyton
Make meal plans for the week for the family.	Volunteer at kids' schools one time per week.	Do own laundry.	Help clean up dinner a couple times per week.	Feed dog in evening.
Volunteer with local Rotary Club a couple times during the week.	Volunteer at church one time per week.	Care for pet rabbit.	Feed dog each morning.	Be respectful to parents.
Do own laundry.	Make doctor, dentist, and haircut appointments for kids.	Be respectful to parents.	Be respectful to parents.	Help fold laundry.
Grocery shop.	Do laundry for self, Brandon, and Peyton.	Clean bathroom once per week.	Mow flat part of lawn.	Go grocery shopping with dad.

Rights				
Jed	Leslie	Molly	Brandon	Peyton
Alone time	Alone time	Alone time	Alone time	Alone time
Time to exercise	Time to exercise	Clean sheets	Clean sheets	Clean sheets
Respect from kids	Respect from kids	Clothes that fit	Clothes that fit	Clothes that fit

175

Privileges				
Jed	Leslie	Molly	Brandon	Peyton
Night out with friends	Girls' night out with friends	Play on volley-ball team	Play video games	Time with friends
Time to play boot hockey on neighbor-hood team	Time to read a book	Time with friends	Time with friends	Playing on basketball team
Time to read a book	Time to watch TV	Talking on phone	Playing on hockey, baseball, and soccer teams	Playing outside
Date night with Leslie	Time to knit	Using cell phone for texts, calls, etc.	Watching TV	Playing video games
	Date night with Jed	Time using social media	Playing outside	Going for a special outing with mom
		Watching TV		

It's difficult to know what responsibilities your child is ready for at different ages. Appendix I includes a chart that can be used as a guideline for what your child is likely ready for, based on her developmental level. Within this, I've included the appropriate expectations for appreciation and gratitude, and when children can begin to take part in various volunteer activities that promote independence and feelings of confidence. This tool can become your guide for independent opportunities for your child through the years.

How Does the Needs-to-Privileges Tool Relate to the Use of Consequences?

When you've presented the Needs-to-Privileges tool to your children, it becomes a form of teaching your child consequences for her behavior, without it feeling like the consequence is being done *to* her. The use of natural and logical consequences will be very effective. If your child decides to take her hat off when she's playing outside in the winter, you can allow her to simply get cold rather than argue with her about how cold she might get. Your child will eventually get cold and realize she needs her hat on. However, if the weather is extremely cold and your child has been sick, the natural consequence won't be appropriate. A logical consequence will need to be used. You might say, "I see you don't want to wear your hat. Since you've been sick and it's so cold out, you won't be able to play outside if you don't wear it. You can wear the red hat or the blue hat, but you need to wear one of these if you're going to go outside."

Your child might still get mad. It's important to stick with your request, despite her possible negative reaction. Your child may attempt to go outside. In this case, you will need to go after your child and walk her (or possibly carry her) back inside. If you give in, she will have learned that your words don't mean anything. If you find you're in this situation often with your child, she's likely seeking power (thinking back to chapter three). This means she's in need of more opportunities that fit in with the *right* kind of power. Learning to manage these behaviors in your child takes time. By remaining patient, taking time to understand her and empowering her through independence, she will gradually gain a sense of responsibility for herself and her actions.

Evaluate Further

At this time, take time to think about the following questions regarding your child:

1. Is my child able to decipher between rights and privileges? How do I know this?

2. When discipline is needed, does my child tend to feel it's being done to her or does she take responsibility for her actions and the results? How can I tell? What could I do to change this?

3. What other adults would I need on board to make these changes?

SECTION FOUR

Discussions

Through this next section on discussions, I will explore with you the importance of having discussions with your family as you navigate this journey.

- *In chapter eight, I will discuss the need for parenting partners to come together to explore issues with the children and family when they arise.*

- *In chapter nine, I'll share insight behind the importance of frequent discussions with your child.*

You will inevitably encounter times where you need course correction. Once you've established your family goals, have an understanding of how children think, are aware of the independence they need, and are able to take the time to regroup with your parenting partner and your child, you'll be on your way to getting back on track.

CHAPTER EIGHT
Parenting Partners
Navigating Together

There are few joys in life as great as seeing the excitement in your child's eyes when she is with someone else who loves her as much as you do. These moments are often shared with a spouse or life partner, or for single parents with a grandparent, close friend, daycare provider, or ex-spouse. I will be referring to all of the above as parenting partners: any adult who helps make parenting decisions with you.

When you're parenting with a partner, it's challenging at times to feel like your beliefs are in line with his or hers. You both have ideas of how you want to raise your child and you bring different life experiences to the table. These differences are good; however, they sometimes make navigating this journey difficult. In chapter one, Where Are We Going?, I discussed how helpful it is to take the time to set family goals and revisit them often. Doing so reminds you and your parenting partner that although your methods for achieving the goals may look different on the outside, your goals are often very similar, if not the same.

You might be in a position where you're parenting with a partner whom you don't live with. This certainly adds another level of challenge to this adventure. Whether living together or apart, a well-working compass is needed.

When Parenting Partners Don't Live Together

When families have experienced separation or divorce, there are sometimes difficult feelings that come out between the two parents. It can be challenging to find the time and the desire to sit down and discuss important parenting topics with your ex-spouse. I discussed, in chapter one, the example of Cara and Drew coming together to discuss their goals and other parenting issues even when it wasn't easy for them emotionally. However, they saw the benefits. For the sake of the children, they made the effort.

If you're separated or divorced from your child's other parent, it's possible you won't be ready to discuss issues in person with your ex-spouse at this time. It may take years to get to this point. The reality is that if you've had a child with another person, that person is forever in your life and a key player in raising your child, even after a divorce. Unless the other parent is harmful to your child, you will want that person involved in your child's life. This will take work and won't be easy, but it's not impossible. It might be beneficial to seek out a third party to help navigate this with you: a family therapist, social worker, or parent consultant are examples. You and your ex-spouse may need to start by communicating by phone to discuss issues until it's easier to be face to face.

It's becoming more common that social service agencies are offering collaborative divorce services for families. Part of this process includes creating a parenting plan with the assistance of a mental health divorce coach. This specialist helps you prioritize the needs of your child through the separation and divorce process, but he or she also includes information for life after the divorce is finalized. A *Even when you're not living with your child's other parent, you still need a compass to help you navigate through life's twists and turns.* parenting plan is a written agreement that provides guidelines for dealing with responsibilities related to your child.

A typical parenting plan outlines the schedule for time with each parent, how to handle vacations and holidays, how to handle a variety of parenting issues that may arise through the years, and how both parties will go about updating this plan in the future. This won't make the pain that often comes with divorce go away, but it will help the process go smoother for the child and will set your family up for success through the years. Even when you're not living with your child's other parent, you still need a compass to help you navigate through life's twists and turns.

Guidance to Carve Out Time

Even when parents do live together, it can still be challenging to find the time to discuss parenting struggles with each other. This was certainly the case for Amy and Josh. The first time I met with Amy and Josh, we made a plan together to help find some ways for their children to get to bed without the struggles that they had been dealing with for the past year. As we finished the first session, both parents admitted that until we talked, they thought they weren't anywhere near being on the same page with their parenting philosophy. However, through defining family goals and in discussing different strategies during our session, they came to realize that they actually had very similar beliefs, but they were just presenting them differently. They had been so frustrated that they had actually stopped talking about how to make things better. Living a frustrated parenting life had become a habit for this couple. I saw a renewed look in their eyes as I said good-bye to them at the end of the meeting.

As I do with most of the families I work with, I met with Amy and Josh a few weeks after our initial session. They said that they went into the next week after our first meeting with energy and excitement, feeling hopeful they could make some changes to help with their children's bedtime struggles. They felt good about their plan, but as more time went on they began to lose their motivation to keep going with the new plan. Plus, they found it hard to carve out the time to sit down together as a couple to discuss various parenting issues and troubleshoot any struggles they encountered when following through with the plan. I hear this from many families: that finding the time to discuss parenting struggles is the biggest challenge.

At the end of my follow-up session with Amy and Josh, they thanked me for providing a time for them to discuss these important issues together. Although I was involved in their discussion, it was truly led by them. With the busy lives that are typical in today's American society, I'm finding that parents need to actually *schedule* time to have focused discussions. Some may want a third party involved simply to hold them accountable until it becomes a habit. Others will be able to carve out discussion time without the involvement of a third party. You need to acknowledge that discussions

When you begin to carve out time for the task of discussing parenting struggles with your parenting partner, you'll be rewarded with a family life that seems to naturally go more smoothly.

should be a high priority. There's no reason why fifteen to thirty minutes can't be set aside each week for parents to touch base and discuss the parenting questions, struggles, or concerns that have come up within their family.

Many parents are great about getting their kids to their sporting or music practices on time and scheduling play time with friends for their children, yet they don't always take the time to sit down with their parenting partners to talk about their children and any issues they're encountering. It's amazing how priorities can so quickly become disjointed. When you begin to carve out time for the task of discussing parenting struggles with your parenting partner, you'll be rewarded with a family life that seems to naturally go more smoothly. You'll also find that you and your parenting partner will fight less and discuss more.

Setting Family Priorities

In his 2007 book *Insightful Parenting*, psychologist Dr. Steven Kahn recommends that families create their schedules surrounding the most important aspects of family life first: time for dinners together, time for discussions, and time for the children to do chores and homework. Once parents have these items established on their calendar, they can add in extras: sports for the kids, visiting with friends, and piano lessons are examples. Often parents schedule the extras first and then scramble to find time for all the *necessary* aspects of family life. If you're doing this, you're inadvertently teaching your child that these other activities are of more importance than family time. Your family is likely your top priority and it's fair to assume you want your child to know this.

Actually following through and making your family your top priority is difficult. I've struggled with this myself at times and certainly struggle to help families figure out ways to do this as well. It's beneficial to have your child involved in a variety of activities throughout the years; however, if these activities get in the way of quality family time, then you'll want to make changes. This might mean taking a break from sporting activities for a while or perhaps even scheduling fewer activities for yourself. When things aren't going well, they won't get better on their own. You have to take the time, with your parenting partner, if you hope for improvement.

There will be times throughout your parenting journey that other things may have to take priority over family life briefly: adjusting to a new job, caring for an ill parent, or focusing on your own mental health are examples. However, if you don't have your family compass in hand, you may not be able to navigate your way back when life calms down again. Your compass will lead you back to your family goals and putting your family first again.

Getting Both Parents on Board for the Journey

Lydia Hamoc and I met once a month to discuss various questions she had about her children. Her spouse, Mac, was unable to join us for the meetings, but Lydia was still happy to get the information she felt she needed. She said she always intended to share the tips and suggestions with Mac, but they never seemed to have time. She was beginning to feel very frustrated that she was taking time to make changes all by herself. She knew she didn't really have a right to be upset since she hadn't shared the tips and suggestions with Mac yet. When I asked why they didn't have time to discuss all of this, she went into a long description of their schedule. Mac worked until about 6:30 p.m. every night and by the time he got home, Lydia was either driving the children to their sporting events or they were sitting down to dinner. Although dinner wasn't always rushed, they had four children, ages four to ten, so there was often a lot of commotion. On the nights they were able to have dinner together, it usually was followed by working on school projects, getting the kids ready for bed, or Lydia leaving for an evening work meeting. Most nights after the kids went to bed, either Lydia was at work or both she and Mac had work to do at home: some of which was for volunteer commitments, some for work, and some household chores. If they had the ability to sit down together, they were often so tired they simply watched TV.

The Hamocs definitely lived a very full life. However, as more time went on, Lydia admitted that she felt really disconnected from Mac. Although he was involved with the kids, she often felt like she was still parenting alone. He usually didn't take an interest in making parenting decisions, so most of this fell on Lydia's shoulders. For many years, she accepted this as her role, but she was beginning to realize lately that it wasn't ideal. She saw how it was affecting her relationship with Mac and his relationship with the children.

I encouraged Lydia to find a time that we could meet when Mac could be present. After a few weeks, we finally found a time that worked for all of our schedules. Mac was supportive and agreed that he should be more involved; however, he wondered how he could find the time. They established their family goals in that meeting, although Lydia had already written a few out when she and I had met previously.

We also talked about their weekend schedule and decided that might be the time they could fit in a thirty-minute meeting to touch base regarding their children. They decided that the children often were busy watching TV together from 9 to 10 a.m. on Saturday mornings, so they could meet then. They previously used that time to clean, but they decided they could clean later in the day.

After listening to Lydia and Mac talk about their concern about being able to find time to discuss into their schedule, I began to worry they might actually decide at the last minute they could clean and talk at the same time instead of sitting down to actually discuss like we planned. I realized that thirty minutes was too much of a stretch when they weren't in the habit of setting time aside to talk about their family life. We decided to set the goal that they would begin to meet every Saturday morning for ten minutes and that they could gradually build upon this. Eventually, they would want enough time to discuss the week's struggles and successes.

For the first month, I sent a text to both Lydia and Mac every Saturday morning at 8:30 reminding them about their goal (we agreed to this beforehand). After a month, we got together one more time to discuss how it had been going. The couple seemed more relaxed at this meeting than they had been at our previous encounter. They were excited to share the brainstorming they had done and the changes that had come out of their conversations. Overall, they felt closer to each other, which also had a positive influence on their family life. They were still working on eliminating some of the weeknight craziness to have more downtime as a family. They still felt they had more things to work on with their kids, but they felt hopeful about their relationship and their schedule. I decided it was time to introduce the idea of family meetings to Lydia and Mac.

CHAPTER NINE
Discussions with Children

So often when parents have issues with their children, they try to parent above them. In other words, they attempt to solve the problem without involvement from the children. Imagine if your boss had an issue with you and she tried everything possible to fix this issue, but she never once had a conversation with you about it. It likely wouldn't get fixed, at least not to the extent it would if she had addressed the issue with you directly.

The Hamoc family, who you met in chapter eight, has four children: two boys and two girls. The children are all doing well in school, have friends, and enjoy being active. However, it's rare that the children get along with each other. This has been a point of frustration for Lydia and Mac for many years, and it seems to be getting worse. Lydia has tried numerous things such as rearranging bedrooms in their house, taking away toys they are fighting over, and grounding them for not getting along. However, none of these tactics really have made a difference.

Family Meetings

I've always been a big supporter of family meetings. This is something my family did throughout my childhood, so I experienced firsthand what they did for my family and how they made me feel as a child. In chapter six, I discussed the importance of children feeling like they have some power and control. I discussed the *right* kind of power and the *wrong* kind of power. Family meetings fall into the category of the *right* kind of power. As a child, I felt valued and respected during these meetings, which carried over into how I felt about my parents and the issues we spent time discussing. For the most part, my siblings and I offered our parents respect in return for how respectful they were to us in these meetings.

Sometimes a family meeting may be a one-on-one discussion with one of your children. For example, when my children were showing signs that they were ready to be toilet trained, around age two, I sat them down to discuss how the process would look. We discussed that we would go out to buy some underwear that they could pick out at the store. I also told them what day we would begin the process. If my children were older, I would have asked them to pick a day within a couple days' window of time that we would start. We would have also discussed how they might want to be reminded that it was time to use the bathroom: a timer or a clock or a different way. Toilet training quickly became a thing the children were a part of rather than something that was being done to them.

Other times family meetings should be held with the whole family or one parent and the children, depending on the issue being addressed. There are some key components that should be included during all family meetings.

Guidelines for Family Meetings

- Always have a piece of paper and pencil or pen to write down the ideas that are discussed. When a child sees his parent write down his ideas, he sees that his ideas are valued, even if he's unable to read at the time.

- Write down even silly ideas that might get brought up.

- Keep an open mind and avoid arguing or getting defensive during these meetings. If you move into command mode, your child will shut down and will no longer feel respected and open to the discussion.

- When you begin the meeting, be sure that your child (and you) are in the Level Head Stage of Control (see chapter four), especially if you're addressing difficult issues.

- End the meeting by summarizing the discussion. If a new plan was made, summarize that as well.

The Hamoc Family Meeting

When it was time for the Hamoc family to sit down with their children to address the issue of sibling rivalry, they were set with their pencil and paper. Lydia and Mac established that the children were all in the Level Head Stage of Control, which they knew was needed for a successful family meeting. They were ready to make a new plan for this family struggle.

Mac decided to lead the meeting. Beyond having a piece of paper to write on, he also had a large piece of tagboard attached to the wall and some markers sitting next to the tagboard. He decided to pass a small sheet of paper out to each of the family members. They were instructed to write one nice thing about everyone in the family. Lydia was ready to help their youngest child as he was just beginning to learn to write. Ruby, their six-year-old, giggled and said, "Does it have to be nice? I don't have anything nice to say about you-know-who." Then she winked in the direction of her little brother, Ricky. Mac didn't react like Ruby was hoping for. He simply repeated the directions, "Write one nice thing about each member of the family." The kids took about ten minutes to do this and then they shared their thoughts. Lydia made her list ahead of time so she was available to help Ricky write his list. Although the two older children had more thought-out answers than the younger children, they all had at least thought of one thing that they liked about each member of the family. The children enjoyed hearing what their siblings had to say about them, but they were equally excited to share their lists with the family.

Next, Mac explained that he and Lydia felt strongly that there needed to be a change in how the children got along with each other. He asked them to list what was going well in their sibling relationships right now. Lydia and Mac added things to the list as well. The following are some examples of items that they included on their list.

The Hamoc family's list of what was going well with their sibling relationships:

- "Michael is sometimes good about sharing his books and toys with me," Monica, age eight

- "Ricky likes to give hugs to everyone in the morning," Michael, age ten

- "I like sharing a room with Monica," Ruby, age six

- "We like to watch TV together," Michael

- "I love everyone!" Ricky, age four

- "We like the *idea* of playing games together," Monica

- "I see Monica and Michael sticking up for each other when they're out playing with the neighbor kids," Lydia

- "I can tell Ruby and Ricky really look up to Michael and Monica," Mac

Next, they listed the things that were not going well. The following includes some examples of the next list the Hamocs created.

The Hamoc family's list of what was not going well with their sibling relationships:

- "Michael doesn't let me play with him when his friends are here," Ricky

- "Monica's quick to tell me what I'm doing wrong, which makes me really mad," Michael

- "She does that to me too!" Ruby

- "Ruby, you do that to me too!" Ricky

- "So, you're saying you feel criticized by each other," Mac

- "Then we usually yell or hit," Michael

- "Ricky always gets into my things. I hate that," Ruby

- "I guess we're not usually all that nice to each other," Monica

- "It feels like you don't like each other most of the time," Lydia

As they were sharing what wasn't going well, there was some uncertainty about the direction the meeting might go as some of the kids got a little defensive. Mac reminded them that this was going to help them solve the issues, even though some of these things were difficult to hear.

When the discussion started to become disrespectful among the siblings, he decided it was time to move to the next question. "What things could we do to help you get along better? What can Mom and I do, what can you four do?" he asked. Lydia spoke first and said she wished she had more one-on-one time with each of the kids. The kids all agreed, so they wrote the idea down. Michael said sometimes they were just arguing and not fighting. He wondered why arguing wasn't okay. They discussed the difference between the two and agreed that arguing isn't bad, but it becomes a problem when it turns into a physical altercation or when yelling begins. Ruby said she wished Ricky would stay out of her things. Mac wrote this suggestion down and asked Ruby if she had ideas of how this could happen. Ruby's eyes lit up as she brought her finger to her chin and said, "Maybe I could keep my special toys in a private container and

Ricky has to ask me before he plays with them. Maybe we could make the private container hard for him to open." Mac wrote this idea down.

Ricky said he liked when Michael brought his friends over, but he didn't like that Michael wouldn't let him play with them. Michael scrunched his forehead and agreed that he could be better about that, but he also stated that he didn't think he needed to include Ricky the whole time.

The meeting continued with suggestions for quite some time. When they had a range of ideas and suggestions, they went through the list together and chose four that they all agreed to work on for that week. The three older kids took turns writing these ideas on tagboard and then they helped Ricky, the youngest, write the words for the last one. They chose a place to post this, so they could be reminded. Before they dispersed, Mac had the four kids and Lydia put their hands to the center of the table. He told them to say, "Go Team Hamoc!" at the count of three and lift their hands into the air. They all did this and giggled. As the four kids walked away from the table, they talked about playing together.

Later that night, Lydia reported that Michael, their oldest child, came out of bed to ask her a question well after it was bedtime. She was worried that something was wrong. However, his question was simple. He asked her if she could type up the responses each family member made regarding how they felt about each other. He said he wanted to keep the list of what everyone said about him next to his bed. He then said he had no idea that Ricky looked up to him so much. Michael hugged his mom and said goodnight.

Based on the reports from Mac and Lydia, the Hamoc children felt connected to each other during and after that meeting. They knew they needed to work on their relationships with their siblings and that their parents were doing things to help them succeed. When you feel connected to those who you spend time with, whether it's family members, coworkers, or friends, you're more invested in making those relationships work.

It's ideal for families to have a follow-up meeting to repro-cess their original discussion. The Hamoc family chose to schedule this meeting one week after the first meeting. It was good timing, as the kids were starting to slip into old habits. They revisited the discussion from the previous week, examined whether they achieved their goals, and decided to add two more goals to the tagboard for the upcoming week.

As discussed in the previous chapter, the Hamoc family was living a very full life, so finding time for this family meeting wasn't easy. The first week they decided to skip their typical Saturday afternoon play time with friends to have the meeting. After that, they decided to tie it into their Sunday night din-ner together, as this was typically the least busy night for their family. After the results of the first week, they were certain they wanted to make this a weekly tradition.

With my own family, we try to meet once a week. We have dinners together far more often than this and have numerous other discussions within the week, but our weekly family meet-ing is deliberately set aside for tackling bigger issues. We have a sheet of paper posted in the mudroom where any of us can add our ideas of what we think needs to be discussed at the meeting. It's simply a set time to regroup as a family about the week's happenings.

Day-to-Day Discussions with Your Child

In today's society, many parents could go most of their day barely even talking face to face with their children, especially when they're teenagers. Technology has expanded in many ways. Younger and younger children have access to cell phones and not only communicate with their friends through texting, but also with their parents. Some of this is great. Parents are able to connect with their teenagers when they may not have been able to in the past. It's even possible that teens are sharing more with their parents, since it's not always face to face, than they would have otherwise. However, in some homes this has replaced the majority of face-to-face conversations altogether.

At very young ages, children are being introduced to watching DVDs as they ride in their car and playing with handheld computer devices and smartphones as they wait at the doctor or during their siblings' sporting events. Prior to these technologies, parents would spend time talking to their children in these situations. Now, parents hand their children electronic devices so they will be occupied. These devices are standing in the way of valuable conversations.

In my role as the summer director for a farm enrichment program for children, I have an opportunity to observe numerous families. I often walk children to their cars at the end of the day. Many times a DVD is already playing when the child hops in his car. The child may begin to tell his parent about his day, but then he gets distracted by

I wonder if the happenings of the morning are leaving his brain as Elmo jumps right back in where he left off earlier.

whatever program is on the DVD player. Perhaps this was a day where the child fed an animal for the first time since he started coming to the program or went on an amazing hike in the sprinkling rain as the sun was shining. His mom may attempt to have him continue telling her, but he likely won't respond as he's instantly drawn in by the show on the DVD player. I wonder if the happenings of the morning are leaving his brain as Elmo jumps right back in where he left off earlier. If the DVD player wasn't on, the parent and child would be discussing his day. He might tell his mom how he fell when he tripped on a root of a tree and how he felt when his friend comforted him. He might tell her how excited he was to finally have the nerve to climb the fence or help make the snack with his teacher. However, we'll never really know because the DVD player was on and the opportunity was lost.

When my children were two and three years old, I was planning to take them by myself on a seven-hour road trip to see my sister. I was a little nervous about the experience, but I was also really excited. The morning we were leaving, I was telling my friend about the trip and she said, "You're going to NEED a portable DVD player! You can borrow mine. Here, it's actually in my car." I felt slightly rude, turning her down, but honestly I was excited to take this trip on without the help of a DVD player.

The car ride was not without stress of course, as the children did get uncomfortable sitting in their car seats. There, of course, was some whininess and frustration. However, we made frequent stops along the way, sang songs, talked about their favorite animals and friends, and talked about what we saw out the windows. I know that our memories of this car ride were far more vivid than they would have been if we had a DVD player entertaining my children for the ride.

A couple years ago, the vehicle we purchased came with a DVD player. We almost didn't buy it because of this, but I was excited about some of the other features it came with. Right away we discussed as a family how the DVD player would be used. We have had the car for two years now and have only used the DVD player four or five times, and each of these times was only during a four-hour or longer drive. We have had many travels that have been anywhere between four to nine hours. At ages seven and eight, my children love looking out the window and can enjoy the varied landscapes. We have had some of our most amazing family conversations in the car. I'd hate to be missing out on the opportunities to hear their thoughts and the discussions they have on these long car rides.

When I was a child, my mom's job was to do medical transcription. She was able to do this from home except that she needed to drive into the city every morning to pick up the tapes to transcribe. From the time I was an infant, I went along on these drives with my mom. I loved these drives. I was a child full of wonder, and my mom listened as I asked a variety of questions. In these very young years, I learned the important aspects of give-and-take conversations. I learned to not only explain what I was asking, but I also learned to listen to what my mom had to say about exciting topics. I'm sure there were days that my mom wished she had some distraction for me if she wasn't feeling well or was tired. I'm sure there were moments I wished for this too. However, when devices are used to entertain children, this can quickly become a habit, which leads to missed opportunities.

A couple years ago, I worked with a family that had two very active boys. The boys preferred to be running around instead of sitting down, unless they were being entertained with technology; however, they were old enough to have the expectation that they could sit still long enough to have a conversation. Their parents said that they had been attempting to go out to eat with the boys lately and it had been going really well because they gave them their smartphones to play with. The parents were so proud to be out as a family and not cause commotion in the restaurant. I understood the relief they must have felt to finally be able to go out with their children. However, when I asked them what they hoped dinner out with the boys might be like when the boys are teenagers, they both hoped they would be discussing school, sports, and their friends as they enjoyed the meal together. I told these parents that this wasn't going to be the case. If the children at ages six and seven were allowed to play with their parents' smartphones during a family meal out, they would likely become teenagers who text their friends during family meals in or out, disinterested in the conversations taking place at the table.

When you allow your child to spend more time interacting with technology than with people, he's missing out on chances to build important social skills. More importantly, you need to consider your child's perception of how you feel about him. If you spend time on your phone checking email or sending text messages while you wait with your child for his doctor appointment rather than spending time talking to him, he will begin to feel as though he

When you allow your child to spend more time interacting with technology than with people, he's missing out on chances to build important social skills.

is less important to you than your work or social life. Your child needs to know that you want to be a part of his life. By talking with him and not allowing technology to interfere more times than not, you'll send the message that you care for him and want to hear his thoughts.

Evaluate Further

As we finish the fourth section, Discussions, take time to think about the following questions:

1. **At this point, how am I making time for quality parenting discussions with my parenting partner?**

2. **How could I make more time for this?**

3. **What things would I want to address during these discussions?**

4. What types of discussions do I currently have with my child on a daily basis?

5. How could I incorporate more?

6. How has this changed as my child has grown?

7. Have I ever had a family meeting before? If so, how did it go? What were the reactions and outcomes after the meeting?

Enjoyment

In this section, I'll discuss the importance of enjoying this journey with your family. Not every day will be enjoyable, of course, as you will naturally encounter struggles. However, there are things you can do to help create joy in your family life more often than not. Without enjoyment, you might lose your motivation to keep going when things get tough. It's a key component to having a well-working compass. At the end of this section, I briefly summarize the *GUIDE* acronym and how you can use this daily with your family.

CHAPTER TEN
Are We Actually Supposed to Enjoy This Journey?

When I met with Cate and Ty a couple years ago, they were thrilled to gain some insight concerning their children. They had been struggling with their one- and three-year-old sons, James and Trevor. They admitted that they had been in survival mode for much of their parenting years. When I asked them what they enjoyed about parenting, they looked at me stunned and said, "Are we actually supposed to be enjoying this?" I laughed, thinking this was a joke, but they remained serious. My feelings quickly moved to sadness. They explained that since things had been so hard for them with the kids, that it was difficult to enjoy this time in their life.

Both Cate and Ty admitted that they really weren't "kid"

people. When they envisioned having children, they pictured being parents of older children. They weren't even sure what young children liked to do or what they were even capable of doing. They felt that having children really had put their lives on hold, and they secretly longed for their old lives back.

In talking with Cate and Ty, it became obvious that they needed to make some changes. I decided to spend some time with them simply discussing what young children are capable of and how this relates to what they could do together as a family. I felt like things would naturally go better in all areas if they had a basic understanding of child development and learned how to enjoy their children more.

I had them create a list of things they enjoyed doing. Ty's list consisted of fishing, hiking, and building things. Cate's list consisted of hiking, reading, and knitting. We decided to start by focusing on hiking and how they could incorporate their children into this hobby.

When the first child, Trevor, was born, they had purchased a backpack that very young children can ride in on the parent's back. They had used it a couple times, but it never felt like they could hike for very long. Since the second child arrived, they hadn't even tried. They hoped someday they would be able to hike as a family. I explained to them that this could happen now, but they just needed to define hiking differently while the children were young. We talked about places they could go for short hikes, where the one-year-old could be in the backpack, but perhaps walk some of the way and the three-year-old could explore. We discussed what amount of time would be fair to expect children these ages to last on a hike. We talked about what young children gain from being outdoors and spending time in nature with their parents. Cate and Ty started to get excited about this. I told them that if the children grew accustomed to hiking with them now, they would be ready for longer hikes in just a few years.

We also discussed how Ty could begin to teach Trevor how to fish. Ty assumed a child would need to be much older than three to do this. Part of what Ty liked about fishing is that it's somewhat of a solitary activity, but he also thought it would be a great way to spend time with his sons. He asked if I thought there was a way his sons could be involved in his building projects, as he missed having time to do this. We talked about having Trevor pass Ty hand tools while Ty worked on projects. I explained to Ty that he could also begin to teach Trevor how to hammer. Perhaps he could even set up a little workbench next to his workstation for Trevor. Trevor could certainly begin to hammer nails into pieces of wood with supervision.

Cate was excited to hear that Trevor was also old enough to learn about knitting, although he was likely not old enough to learn how to actually knit. She had assumed a young child wouldn't be interested in this and would likely only make a mess of the project rather than listen and watch. We discussed how Trevor could help her pick out which colors to use and could possibly try something *like* knitting as he sat next to her: using string lacing cards or beads or pushing a blunt needle with yarn through Styrofoam trays.

We also talked about the benefits that kids gain from seeing their parents read for pleasure, assuming the parents still read to the children at other times. Cate felt like she finally had permission to do some of the things she loved, even during her time caring for the children. She assumed it had to be all about the kids, but she didn't know what that was supposed to look like.

I continued to check in with the couple for a few months. Ty had taken Trevor fishing once and they had a great time. They were both excited to go again. Ty was in the midst of building a workbench for Trevor and decided to make it large enough so James could use it when he was old enough. Cate sat down with Trevor to show him her knitting needles and yarn. He was very intrigued and asked if she could make him a scarf. She was thrilled that he was excited about this and of course started making him his scarf. Although there were still moments when they were unsure of how to interact with their children, it was beginning to be more natural. The bottom line is that they began enjoying their parenting journey more.

We decided to continue meeting for a while to talk more about basic child development, so they could anticipate the different stages their children would go through and when they might be ready for other family activities. Even before this, Cate and Ty noticed positive changes in their home life and with the boys' behaviors. Simply stepping back to assess how they could alter their family life in positive ways helped them enjoy this journey more.

Schedules Getting in the Way: One Family's Story

Earlier in the year, I met a good friend for lunch. As she sat down, she let out a big sigh. I asked if everything was okay and she said it was fine, but she had overcommitted herself. She explained all that she had going on with work, volunteer commitments, and helping her mom care for her ill father. I asked how her kids were. She sighed again and said, "I think they're pretty good, but I'm so busy I don't even really know." She explained how lately she wasn't feeling much joy when she was with them. She used to love hearing their stories about school and about funny things their friends would say or do. She said this wasn't the case anymore. She said she wanted to enjoy them, but it just didn't feel like it was in her.

We then talked about how unbalanced our lives can get and what we can do to change things. Suddenly, my friend looked at me and said, "I can change this!" She went on to explain that if she really wanted to enjoy her children more, she could make some changes. She couldn't change her work schedule right now and her mom really needed her help. She loved her volunteer work, but she knew deep down the group she was volunteering for would be okay if she stepped back for a bit. It wouldn't be permanent, just enough to refocus and spend time genuinely engaging with her children again. My friend got up at this moment, tossed some money on the table, gave me a quick hug, and took off.

She was so thankful she finally acknowledged that she had some control over her schedule.

A month later, I ran into this friend again while we were both running errands with our children. I asked how things were going, and she said they were much better. She was so thankful she finally acknowledged that she had some control over her schedule. This friend luckily had a very good relationship with her children, and prior to her busier schedule she had spent time equipping her family with a well-working compass. It didn't take them long to reconnect. In fact, her children likely didn't even notice her lack of enjoyment. However, *she* noticed and knew she wanted it to be different.

Change Created More Enjoyment: Another Family's Story

A few months ago, after teaching a class, I was talking with some of the parents who were in attendance. There was a mom standing off to the side who appeared to be waiting for a turn to talk to me. When the room cleared a bit, this mom, Rianne, approached me. She explained that she had two children, ages four and five, who simply exhausted her. She seemed embarrassed to admit this. I asked her what aspects were exhausting to her. She went on to tell me that they refused to dress themselves and clean up their toys and always wanted her to entertain them. Her eyes filled with tears as she said, "I couldn't wait to be a mom and I'm trying to do everything I can for them, but it's just not fun. I don't like this." I put my hand on her shoulder and told her that we could make it better. She took my number and called me the next morning to set up a time to meet.

"I couldn't wait to be a mom and I'm trying to do everything I can for them, but it's just not fun. I don't like this."

When Rianne and I met a couple weeks later, we started by reviewing what her children were capable of learning how to do on their own, so we could take some of the pressure off of her. I introduced the idea of family meetings to her, so she had a means of sharing the idea that things needed to be different with the children. Rianne was relieved to hear that it was okay to tell her children to play on their own and that she didn't need to entertain them all the time.

Rianne met with the kids about some household tasks they could begin to do. As you read in chapter six, children love to feel independence and know that the adults in their lives believe in them when they're given responsibilities. Even though the kids acted like they wanted their mom to do everything for them, it's not what's natural to young chil- *Even though the kids acted like they wanted their mom to do everything for them, it's not what's natural to young children.* dren. Young children love to be helpful and know they're a part of something bigger than themselves. Unfortunately, Rianne's children had learned to be helpless. When Rianne explained to the children that their family life didn't feel very fun lately and that she needed help from the kids to make this better, they were willing to take on some responsibilities.

I got a call from Rianne a month after we met. She wanted to thank me for our time together. She said she couldn't believe how different their household felt. The kids were gradually taking on more responsibilities, were dressing themselves, and were beginning to play on their own more. She said she was finally finding time for some of her own hobbies. Since she had time to herself and didn't feel like her children's constant playmate, she felt rejuvenated when it was time to be with them. Since the children were young, they unlearned their helpless behavior quickly. This journey had become something Rianne enjoyed. She had hoped for this for years.

One Mom's Perspective through Challenging Times

My friend Michelle has had a unique perspective while raising her children. When Michelle met her husband, Beau, he was a single parent to an eleven-year-old girl, Alexa. Michelle got to know Alexa very well. By the time Michelle and Beau got married a few years later, Alexa was approaching her mid-teens. Michelle had certainly become a big part of Alexa's life. Michelle was in awe of how quickly her stepdaughter was growing up.

Two years after Michelle and Beau got married, they had their first child together, Lanie. Soon after Lanie was born, they realized she had acid reflux. She was very uncomfortable and needed to be held most of the time. There were many nights Lanie would cry through the night. I had gone through something similar with my son only two years prior to this and remember talking to Michelle about how difficult it was. Michelle agreed it was hard, but she admitted that she actually enjoyed that time with Lanie in the middle of the night. She said she knew, from her time with Alexa, that Lanie would grow fast and some day, in the not-so-distant future, she wouldn't need to be held through the night anymore.

Through Lanie's toddler and preschool years, she encountered some other health issues: constant ear infections, colds, and other upper respiratory infections. These illnesses are very normal for children, but it seemed Lanie's lasted longer and were more frequent. The family had to carve out time for doctor visits, which led to many missed days of work for Michelle and missed play dates for Lanie. Of course, Michelle wished her daughter wasn't getting sick so often, as it was hard to see her daughter that way.

However, despite the challenges these illnesses brought, Michelle always had a smile on her face and stayed positive. Michelle continued to hold Lanie when she needed it and took the nighttime waking in stride, as she knew this time in their life would go fast. She went beyond getting *through* the moment, to actually enjoying it.

As Michelle's family has grown, with the addition of Eddie four years after Lanie, Michelle has continued to have this perspective. Alexa is now in the midst of college, and although they still have a close relationship, she doesn't have the same needs as the younger children. Michelle knows some day, in the not-so-distant future, Lanie and Eddie will be off at college too. I have admired Michelle's perspective for many years now and wish I would have had a little bit more of this when my children were babies, when they woke frequently through the night or needed constant holding through the days.

How Goals, Understanding, Independence, and Discussions Affect Enjoyment

I've shared numerous stories throughout the book of how families made changes, some big and some small, but all of which led to a more enjoyable family life. Not every day will be enjoyable, of course, but if there are more days that aren't than days that are, it's time to make a new plan. Since you're at this point in the book, you're already on the road to a more enjoyable journey.

First of all, people often feel happier when they're living

with purpose. By taking time to set family goals and examining the type of relationship you hope to have with your child, you'll naturally begin parenting with more purpose. You now have the tools to focus your priorities to have the family life you've hoped for. This plan may look very different for each family, but being able to raise your child with purpose is one of the greatest beauties in life.

When you begin to understand those around you, especially those whom you're entrusted to care for, you'll also find greater enjoyment in life. Your child will be happiest when she feels understood. When a child is constantly having tantrums and challenging her parents to try to get her way, she's not truly enjoying life. The child, being rewarded for her tantrums by getting what she wants, may think she's happy. This isn't true happiness, though. Helping your child find the right balance of control and power to be the independent soul she needs to be to grow up is what will lead to greater fulfillment in her life and allow her to become a productive member of society. It isn't until your child feels *genuine* happiness and confidence that she will experience *true* joy. There is so much comfort in being surrounded by those who truly know you, love you, and are there to help you become the best you that you can be.

It's important for families to have fun together. You naturally feel more connected to those you've created happy memories with. These moments can be going on family trips together, hiking together, playing board games together, doing yard work together, or simply watching a movie together, as a family. If it doesn't seem like this is happening at this point in your life, take time to discuss with your parenting partner and/or your child how you can connect more.

Evaluate Further

Take time to think about the following questions:

1. What do I enjoy most about being a parent?

   - How is this different from what I thought it would be prior to becoming a parent?

   - How is this the same?

2. What does my family currently enjoy doing together?

3. What are some other activities that I think my family would enjoy doing together?

- Could we do these now or will we need to wait until the children are older?

- If we need to wait, what things are similar that my younger children could do now?

4. What might be preventing me from enjoying my child and this journey? How can I change this?

As you complete *Your Family Compass*, I hope you'll continue to come back to it throughout your child's years. In the first section, Goals, you had the opportunity to think about the values and characteristics you hope your child will have through the years, along with the type of relationship you hope to have with her now through adulthood. These goals help you remember that it's important to parent for the long term, rather than simply for the moment. You were introduced to the idea of Family Mission Statements to express what your family strives to achieve together. All of these goal-setting activities create a foundation for your family to work off of. Some people could argue that your goals alone could be your compass. Although I agree that these are the core for your compass, the other components are still imperative.

In the second section, Understanding, you learned how children learn and think, why they behave the way they do, what makes them who they are, and how you can react to their behaviors and temperament. Without this understanding, there's uncertainty. If you're unaware of what is developmentally appropriate at different ages, you might think something is terribly wrong with your child or be unsuspecting of concerns. Not every aspect of development was covered in the Understanding section; however, this basic understanding is enough to create a framework for you to work off of.

In chapter five, It's About Learning, I discussed the importance of remembering that not only is your child learning throughout this process, but so are you. You will make mistakes. They're inevitable. In these moments, you can apologize to your child, if necessary, and make adjustments to attempt to avoid the mistake in the future. Most of all, you need to forgive yourself and move forward.

Throughout the third section, Independence, I talked about the human need to have power and control. It's not always easy to identify between the *right* kind and the *wrong* kind of power and control. However, when you have a deeper understanding of why independence is necessary and how children interpret autonomy, you're better equipped to decipher between the two kinds of power and control and choose appropriately for your child.

Most parents have many questions about discipline. Earlier in the book, I shared the difference between discipline and punishment. Discipline is teaching or giving instruction, whereas punishment is inflicting pain or harm for an offense. Inflicting punishment on the child may extinguish the negative behavior, but it won't get to the root of the cause. When your approach to parenting can move from extinguishing behaviors to actually teaching through discussions (section four), you'll find this journey to be more rewarding. Your child will feel more on board with the decisions made and will be less likely to push back on your requests.

Have you ever enjoyed a wonderful conversation with a dear friend that you wish could last forever? When you start having discussions with your child when he's young, he learns important conversational skills that will help him throughout life. He'll also learn respect for his family and gain an understanding of the ability to grow more connected to others through discussions. He will respect what you say because you've shown him respect for what *he* has to say. Someday that conversation that you wish could last forever could be with your child.

Discussions are the means for putting the other aspects—

Goals, Understanding, and Independence—into practice. When you're taking time to have discussions with your parenting partner regarding various family issues (positive and negative), you'll have a stronger sense of how to move forward with your decisions. They provide an opportunity to analyze if course correction is necessary. Sometimes, even the simple act of a discussion with your family sets you back on your family's intended course.

Enjoying your children will often happen naturally when the above aspects have been addressed. Sometimes it's as simple as gaining a different perspective. Many times, even within the challenging times, there is a gift or a lesson to be learned. When you're able to move through life with this perspective, you'll be more patient and able to see the joy despite the struggle.

Continue to take this GUIDE with you through the various stages of your family life. Frequently review the responses to the workbook portions that you filled out throughout the book. Set aside family time to pursue these ideas throughout your child's years. Even when your child is a teen and spending more time with her friends, keep family time a priority. Your child will thank you in the future.

Take the GUIDE visual with you in your mind as you continue to navigate this journey with your family. You can ask yourself the following questions:

G   Am I parenting toward my family Goals?

U   Do I have an Understanding of my child, and am I helping him begin to understand himself?

I   Am I providing a variety of opportunities for Independence for my child?

D   Do I have quality Discussions with my parenting partner and child?

E   Am I Enjoying our family life more often than not?

Occasional difficulties with children are inevitable. There's no way to be ready for everything that comes your way as a parent, and you'll often find yourself on paths of uncertainty. This is life. It happens to us, whether we want it to or not. Keep your family compass in your hand and I promise you with time, you'll find your way.

ACKNOWLEDGMENTS

I always hoped I'd write a book someday. In fact, as a child I dreamt of being an author of children's stories. I spent many days during my childhood writing. My best friend, Nancy Ngo, illustrated many of my stories. We had grand plans of being a dynamic duo: I'd be the writer and she'd be the illustrator. These stories never went anywhere, not even the story of *Scott and Friends* that I wrote from ages eight to eleven and actually included more than two hundred pages. As I grew from a child into an adolescent, I realized I was really meant to be a teacher. As I'm finishing up this project, it's fun to think that although this book is far from *Scott and Friends*, I was still able to fulfill part of my childhood dream of becoming an author.

As I've worked with families over the course of the past few years, parents started to ask me when I would write my own book. I usually laughed it off saying I was too young and I needed to wait until my children were older (more proof that it worked, right?). However, the more people asked, the more I started to wonder. In the spring of 2011, two women, on separate occasions, pulled me aside and said, "I think the time for you to do this is now." It was these words that gave me the push and confidence to jump into the project. I'm grateful for the encouragement these two women, Anna Rusch and Liz McGinley, gave me to take this on . . . and not just someday, but now!

I was graciously welcomed into a writers' group soon after I had made my decision to start writing. These women—Meagan Franke, author of *Choosing to Grow Through Marriage*; Sue Swanson; Laura Moyer; and Anja Kuehne-Welsh—guided me through a process I really knew nothing about, from publishing options to how to work through the uncertainty of where to take a chapter. They occasionally read through some of my work and provided helpful feedback for me to work with. Mostly, I appreciated their support and guidance.

There were many others, though, who helped talk me through different publishing options and literary possibilities. These conversations were incredibly important for me on this journey. Thank you to Sue Baldwin, Derek Wolden, Erik Hildebrandt, Heather Zenzen, Alison Behnke, Colleen Baldrica, and Dr. David Bredehoft. Also a special thanks to Jody Nyehnuis and Dave Jacobson for taking the time to talk to me about possible title and analogy ideas.

In the summer of 2011, I gathered a group of my friends—Kim Corbett, Tonia Theroux, Amy Pundsack, Becky Biederman, Lisa Warner, Trupti Storlie, and Suzanne McDowell—to share my book idea and brainstorm titles. Although the title I walked away with on that night is not my final one, this process was very helpful to me. It was wonderful to hear feedback from these friends and hear the excitement they had for the concept of the book. I began officially writing then in September 2011, the first day back at school for my kids after their summer break.

I dove into my writing with two feet. Essentially, my goal was to pull information from one of the classes for parents I had been teaching for years to put into a book. As more time went on, though, the book took on far more than I would have imagined. By that winter, I had a pretty comprehensive manuscript. At that time, I had eight people read through it to provide feedback on the content and the ability to apply it to everyday parenting. I'm forever grateful to these eight people: Lisa Warner, Kim Corbett, Chuck McGinley, Patti Hanlon, Jason Hanlon, Becky Biederman, Liz McGinley, and Tonia Theroux. Prior to this stage, Tonia had also helped me with some editing early in the process. Her insight into writing and the project itself was immeasurable.

There were others beyond the above eight and my writers' group who had eyes on portions of the manuscript prior to it going into editing. Thank you to Kelly Herbster, Donna McGinley, Shelly Rock, Stefanie Lorinser, Kim Brown, and Vicky Greene. Even if they only read a chapter or two, the feedback received was very beneficial for this process.

As I moved into the next phase of the project, I began looking at cover designs. Amanda Hanlon was incredibly patient with me through this process, as I changed titles and thoughts on how I wanted the cover to look. All of these changes were positive, although it made things stressful along the way. It means a lot to me to have Amanda, my sister-in-law, design my cover. Also, a special thanks to LeAnne Schmidt of Photog Frog for taking the perfect photo for this cover! Many friends have had eyes on the various cover design options and provided me with feedback. Thank you to Lynn and Paul Weitzel, Karlyn Peterson, Ken and Liz McGinley, Tonia and Brent Theroux, Carrie Rickheim, Kim Corbett, Chuck McGinley, Mike McGinley, and Kelly Herbster, along with many of those listed above.

I'm very grateful to have been connected with Beaver's Pond Press. From the first time I met with Dara Beevas, I felt like this publishing company was going to be the best fit for me. Lily Coyle had a crucial role in this process, as she has guided me through the intricacies of publishing a book—from tears in her office the first time we went through my manuscript together, to laughing and talking together over the phone about how much easier the process gets once the book is actually written. Her mentoring through this process was exactly what I needed to get my book to where I wanted it to be. Thank you to Leah Noel my editor and Molly Miller my proofreader for working with me on my manuscript. And, thank you to Jay Monroe for working with me on the interior design of the book along with the back cover and spine.

I want to say a special thank you to Dr. Marti Erickson for taking time out of her busy schedule to read through my manuscript, provide feedback to me, and write my foreword. I'm honored that she felt this was a project she wanted to support.

Prior to this book writing process, there are people who led me to where I am now in my career. I want to thank Nancy Jones for continuing to be one of my mentors for so many years. So much of who I am as a teacher is the result of the time I have spent with her: watching her teach, mentoring me, and discussing our time together teaching. I greatly admire her passion for quality experiences for children and their parents. She's an amazing woman. I'm honored to have worked with her for so many years at her school, The Children's Farm.

Another woman who has greatly influenced my professional career is Julie Powers. I was all of twenty-four years old when she hired me as one of the founding teachers of Dodge

Nature Preschool. I was young, but highly motivated and determined. She saw this in me and despite the concerns the rest of the hiring committee had about my age, she took a chance on me. I'm so grateful she did, as my time at Dodge was incredible. Julie has always been very supportive of my professional choices and has been a wonderful guide throughout all of it.

In many ways, this book has taken over my life this past year. I've had less time with my friends. Everyone has been so patient as I've had to turn down numerous gatherings, visits for tea or hot chocolate, runs, and more. I've missed my time with friends and am looking forward to having more balance back in my life again. Thank you to all of you who have still encouraged me even though it meant I was a little more absent from your life for a while.

My children and husband have been incredibly patient throughout this process. My husband took over many family and house-related tasks that have typically been my responsibilities. Although work has been busy for him as well, he has taken this all on with very few complaints and has continued to support me. For this, I'm very grateful. Although my children acknowledge that they're excited to have more time with me again (as am I!), they know I'm very passionate about helping families. They understand that the book is another way I can do this. I'm grateful for their patience and ability to see beyond themselves and our family.

I firmly believe that God has been very purposeful by carefully positioning certain people and places into my life. I thank God daily not only for the gifts of my two children, but also for the opportunities I've had as a teacher and parent educator. I also thank God often for giving me the courage to take on a project of this magnitude. There were many times through this process God carried me and provided me stamina when I wasn't sure how I could possibly have done it. There was something bigger than myself pushing this project, and I'm grateful for that.

Last, but not least, I want to thank all of the families I've ever worked with. I've had the pleasure of teaching so many children through the years, and each one has influenced me in different ways. I've had the opportunity to also work with many parents through the years. Thank you to all of you who have welcomed me into your homes and lives and for trusting me to be your guide through this journey of parenting.

APPENDIX I

Capabilities Based on Developmental Level to Promote Autonomy

1.5–2.5 Years Old (Toddler Years)

Tasks at this developmental stage are beneficial for your child to feel BIG (competent and confident in his abilities) and for him to see himself as a contributing member of the family.

Self-Care & Personal	Family Responsibilities
• Put clothes in laundry basket when being changed. • Begin to clean up toys. • Wipe up spills.	• Carry cups and plastic dishes over to the counter after meals. • Water plants (use small plastic pitcher). • Begin to help with meal preparation: stirring, cutting up soft fruits and veggies, and pouring ingredients into bowls. • Begin to shovel snow. • Sweep the floor or garage. • Wipe down tables and chairs.
Showing Gratitude	**And Beyond . . .**
• Teach child to say please and thank you. • Model saying thank you. • Casually express your gratitude during the day. Say something like "I'm so thankful it's sunny today!"	• Carry in flowers to someone who needs their day cheered up. • Plant a flower to give to someone. • With parent, help a neighbor or friend by walking their dog or playing with their pet. • Visit a friend, relative, or acquaintance in a nursing home.

2.5–4 Years Old (Preschool Years)

Tasks at this developmental level are similar to those in the toddler years, the stage referenced in the previous category, yet children this age are capable and ready for more detailed tasks. Involvement at this age will really set the stage for your child to be able to take on responsibilities and begin to see the world beyond him-or herself.

All of the above from the previous category, plus the following:

Self-Care & Personal	Family Responsibilities
• Pick up toys after playing with them. • Begin to make bed (simply pulling up covers). • Self-care tasks: dress self, brush teeth, hang coat, etc.	• Dust. • Help to sort laundry. • Put laundry in machine. • Carry laundry to laundry room in basket. • Assist with meal planning and preparation: • Cut veggies and fruit. • Crack eggs. • Feed pets with supervision. • Wipe tables/countertops. • Assist at grocery store with picture list (count how many apples are needed and how many oranges, etc.). Keep list to three to four items for children this age. • Plant seeds, water garden, and begin weeding and harvesting

Showing Gratitude	And Beyond . . .
• Draw thank-you cards when gifts are given or when someone does something kind.	• Make someone a card (someone who might be sick or sad or simply to make a family member or friend smile).
• Expect to say please and thank you.	• Pick out food from cabinet or store to deliver to the food shelf.
• Establish bedtime or mealtime tradition to share gratitude of the day.	• Shovel snow, your own driveway and your neighbors'.
• Model appreciation for everyday things: heat, light, friends, etc.	• Help prepare a meal for someone who needs it.
	• Pick up garbage on a walk.

*** *Children at these ages may be capable of doing and understanding some of the activities that are listed for older children if it's done more on a one-on-one basis, rather than in a large group setting.*

5–6 Years Old

Tasks at this developmental level are more advanced than at the preschool stage, the stage referenced in the previous category, but adult supervision is still necessary. Children in this stage are less egocentric and are even better equipped to see how they can influence the lives of others in positive ways.

All of the above from the previous categories, plus the following:

Self-Care & Personal	Family Responsibilities
• Self-care tasks: bathe self, brush own hair (will still need assistance with this), brush teeth, pick out own clothes, dress self, get snacks/breakfast for self. • Take care of personal items: hang up coat, put shoes away, bring dirty laundry to laundry room, bring own dishes after meals to counter or place directly in dishwasher, put toys away, clean room, put laundry away.	• Begin to wash dishes, load dishwasher, unload dishwasher (with assistance). • Begin to fold laundry. • Push in chair after meals and wipe table, sinks, etc. • Dust. • Feed pets. • Begin to set table. • Help with party prep (preparing name tags for guests at chairs, setting table, etc.). • Assist with grocery shopping: help gather items while in store.

Showing Gratitude	And Beyond . . .
• Keep a family gratitude journal. • Write thank-you notes and mail or deliver in person. • Make a list of things you are grateful for. • Encourage financial generosity: save, share, spend.	• Rake leaves for a family in need. • Save money or collect money for a cause that means something to the child. • Help decorate and create cards for an organization (could be used as thank-you cards for the organization, for example). • Collect food for the food shelf. • Sponsor a family: plan and decide on gifts for the family and shop together for these items.

7–9 Years Old

Tasks at this age are more detailed and require more skill and concentration. The idea would be to do these tasks with your child at first until she is capable of doing them on her own.

All of the above from the previous categories, plus the following:

Self-Care & Personal	Family Responsibilities
• Pack own lunches with guidance and support. • Begin to cook own meals with adult supervision: scramble eggs or brown meat (in electric skillet or electric stove), cut veggies, make salads, measure ingredients, etc.	• Bring out the trash/gather trash into one garbage bag in the house. • Vacuum. • Load and unload dishwasher. • Clear and set table. • Clean mirrors, sink, counters with guidance and only with non-toxic cleaning products. • Shovel snow. • Weed, tend to garden, and harvest with greater independence. • Hand wash and dry dishes.

Showing Gratitude	And Beyond . . .
• Continue to model generosity: let others go ahead of you in line, hold the door for others. Encourage your child to do the same.	• Wash and dry dishes after having a meal at a friend's house as a way to show appreciation for the meal.
	• Gather plates from guests after a meal at your own house to bring to kitchen counter.
	• Ask guests what they would like to drink or take their coats when they arrive.
	• Rather than birthday gifts, host a birthday party with a cause: encourage child to make a donation to a certain cause, collect items to be donated, or do a service project together.
	• Put birthday bags together to be donated to a food shelf.
	• Write a thank-you letter to a soldier or local service professional: police officer, firefighter, teacher, etc.

10–12 Year Olds

Tasks at these ages are to help the overall family system flow as best it can, but also to provide your child with skills that he will need as he continues to grow into someone who will one day live on his own and will desire a life of giving back to his community.

All of the above from the previous categories, plus the following:

Self-Care & Personal	Family Responsibilities
• Keep room presentable. • Take responsibility for getting own laundry to laundry room to be cleaned. • Make sure homework gets done. • Keep track of own stuff.	• Begin to learn how to mow the lawn (child dependent and must be done with adult supervision for the first few times). • Clean toilets and bathrooms with nonchemical-based cleaning products. • Plan and prep meals if needed. • Begin to care for younger siblings (eleven and older; again, child dependent). • Help with younger siblings.

Showing Gratitude	And Beyond . . .
• Write thank-you cards on own when gifts are given or when someone does a kind act.	• Begin to be a mother's helper or babysit (eleven and older for babysitting).
• Thank parents.	• Volunteer to walk neighbor's pet.
• Offer to help parents throughout the house even without being asked and beyond the typical responsibilities.	• Care for neighbor's pet when owners are on vacation.
	• Offer to help a neighbor carry in groceries.

12–15 Year Olds

By this age, children have mastered the self-care tasks and are beginning to learn how to take care of broader responsibilities, such as paying for their cell phone, learning how to use money they earn, et cetera. Many children at these ages want to make a difference and will seek out volunteer opportunities. They may be more inclined to help others beyond their family at these ages. Parents can encourage both.

All of the above from the previous categories, plus the following:

Self-Care & Personal	Family Responsibilities
• Keep track of own schedule and deadlines with adult guidance.	• Continue with the previous household tasks, and also begin to do those things on a larger scale.
• Learn greater personal hygiene.	• Help parents when needed.
• Start to seek out own volunteer and work opportunities.	• Pick out and plan a family fun night each month.
• Learn the difference between a want and a need.	• Help care for younger siblings.
• Set own alarm to wake in morning and get to bus and school on time.	
• Begin to do laundry on own with adult guidance.	
• Make time to develop a hobby.	
Showing Gratitude	**And Beyond . . .**
• Thank friends for their friendship.	• Seek meaning in life.
• Send thank-you cards at the end of a semester to the teachers.	• Organize volunteer or service projects with friends, such as a neighborhood closet cleaning day. Deliver everything collected to a thrift store.

APPENDIX 2

Helpful Phrases for Child Guidance

- "I can see you thought it was a good idea to take out the blocks right now. However, I was just coming over to tell you we have to clean up for dinner. We can play with these later today."

- "I know you really want to take that hike today, but we just don't have time. When we get home let's write down that we will make time for that hike in the next week."

- Child is painting at an easel inside and says, "Mom, can we paint outside?" Mom could respond, "I hadn't thought about that. I think it's a perfect day for that. Yes!"

- "I realize that every day you ask if you can have grilled cheese for lunch. We've been so busy that we haven't been able to have it in a while. Let's put it on the calendar that we will make it this weekend."

- "I can tell you really like helping me. Would you like to wash the dishes after lunch?"

- "You see me dusting and want to help too. I'll get you a towel and I'll show you where you can start. Thanks!"

- "What's your plan?"

APPENDIX 3

Behavior Assessment and Action Plan

I.   What is the issue?

2.   Why is this a problem?

3.   **Why is this happening?** (temperament, age, frustration, goals for or causes of behavior, other)

4. What do I want my child to learn from this?

5. How do I best teach this so my child internalizes the expected behavior for the long term?

6. What are some current obstacles for teaching this? (time, schedule, other)

7. How will I address these obstacles?

APPENDIX 4

Words of Encouragement

- "I know you can do it."

- "You've almost got it."

- "It's hard. I'll sit by you while you continue to try."

- "I remember when I was learning how to do that too."

- "Let's try it together."

- "I'm tired too, but we're almost there."

REFERENCES

American Academy of Pediatrics. "The FITT Plan for Physical Activity." *Care of Young Athlete* patient education handouts. Washington, D.C.: American Academy of Pediatrics, 2011.

Bentzen, W. R. *Seeing Young Children: A Guide to Observing and Recording Behavior.* New York: Delmar Publishers, 1993.

Boeree, C. G. "Abraham Maslow." Shippensburg University, Pennsylvania. Accessed in 2006. http://webspace.ship. edu/cgboer/maslow.html.

Bravo, E. *The Job/Family Challenge.* New York: John Wiley & Sons, 1995.

Bredehoft, D., J. Illsley Clarke, and C. Dawson. *How Much Is Enough?* Cambridge, MA: Da Capo Press, 2004.

Bronson, P., and A. Merryman. *Nurture Shock: New Thinking About Children.* New York: Twelve, 2009.

Cloud, H., and J. Townsend. *Raising Great Kids: A Comprehensive Guide to Parenting with Grace and Truth.* Grand Rapids, MI: Zondervan, 2000.

Corkille Briggs, D. *Your Child's Self-Esteem.* New York: Dolphin Books, 1975.

Csikszentmihalyi, M. *Flow: The Psychology of Optimal Experience.* New York: Harper & Row, 1990.

Culbert, T., and R. Kajander. *Be the Boss of Your Stress.* Minneapolis: Free Spirit Publishing, 2007.

Curran, D. *Traits of a Healthy Family.* New York: Ballantine Books, 1983.

_____. *Stress and the Healthy Family.* Minneapolis: Winston Press, 1985.

Damon, W. *Greater Expectations: Overcoming the Culture of Overindulgence in America's Homes and Schools.* New York: The Free Press, 1995.

Davis, Laura, and Janis Keyser. *Becoming the Parent You Want to Be.* New York: Broadway Books, 1997.

Doherty, W. J. *Take Back Your Kids.* Notre Dame, IN: Sorin Books, 2000.

Downs, S. "The Other Homework." *St. Paul Pioneer Press*, October 2007.

Dreikurs, Rudolph. *Children: The Challenge.* New York: Hawthorn Books, 1964.

Dreikurs, R., and P. Cassell. *Discipline without Tears: A Reassuring and Practical Guide to Teaching Your Child Positive Behavior.* New York: Dutton, 1972.

Dutwin, D. *Unplug Your Kids.* Avon, MA: Adams Media, 2009.

Eastwood, A. *Adolescence.* Upper Saddle River, NJ: Prentice Hall, 1992.

Elkind, D. *The Power of Play.* Philadelphia: Da Capo Lifelong Books, 2007.

Erickson, M. "Separating Fact from Fiction about Parent-Child Attachment." Accessed 2010. http://www.goodenoughmoms.com.

Faber, Adele, and Elaine Mazlish. *How to Talk so Kids Will Listen and Listen so Kids Will Talk.* New York: Harper Collins, 1980.

_____. *Siblings without Rivalry.* New York: Avon Books, 1987.

Garbarino, J. "Power Struggles: Early Experiences Matter." *Child Care Information Exchange* 55 (2001).

Gardner, H. *The Disciplined Mind.* New York: Simon & Schuster, 1999.

Gartrell, D. "Misbehavior or Mistaken Behavior?" *Young Children*, July 1995.

_____. *The Power of Guidance: Teaching Social-Emotional Skills in Early Childhood Classrooms.* Independence, KY: Wadsworth Publishing, 2004.

_____. "Promote Physical Activity—It's Proactive Guidance." *Young Children,* March 2008.

Goldenthal, P. *Beyond Sibling Rivalry.* New York: Henry Holt & Company, 1999.

Goleman, D. *Emotional Intelligence: Why It Can Matter More than IQ.* New York: Bantam, 2006.

Greenman, J. "Children Need to Live in the Real World." *Child Care Information Exchange* 59 (1995).

Haber, C. C., and Gessell Institute of Human Development. *He Hit Me First: When Brothers and Sisters Fight.* New York: Dembner Books, 1989.

Hamner, T. J., and P. H. Turner. *Parenting in Contemporary Society.* Boston: Allyn & Bacon, 2001.

Henner, M. *I Refuse to Raise a Brat.* New York: Regan Books, 1999.

Hirsch-Pasek, K., and R. M. Golinkoff with D. Eyer. *Einstein Never Used Flashcards.* Philadelphia: Rodale Publishing, 2003.

Hitz, Randy, and Amy Driscoll. "Praise or Encouragement?" *Young Children,* July 1988.

Illsley Clarke, J. *Self-Esteem: A Family Affair.* Minneapolis: Winston Press, 1978.

Illsley Clarke, J., and C. Dawson. *Growing Up Again: Parenting Ourselves, Parenting Our Children.* New York: Harper & Row, 1997.

Jones, Nancy. "Big Jobs and Challenges." *Young Children,* 2004.

Kahn, Steve. *Insightful Parenting.* St. Paul, MN: Family Therapy Press, 2007.

Karp, Harvey. *Happiest Baby on the Block.* New York: Bantam Books, 2003.

Kindlon, D. *Too Much of a Good Thing.* New York: Hyperion, 1984.

Kohn, Alfie. *Punished by Rewards.* New York: Houghton Mifflin Company, 1999.

_____. "Five Reasons to Stop Saying Good Job!" *Young Children,* September 2001.

Kurcinka, Mary Sheedy. *Raising Your Spirited Child.* New York: Harper, 2006.

_____. *Sleepless in America.* New York: Harper Collins, 2006.

Kurdek, L. A. "Nature and Prediction of Changes in Marital Quality for First-Time Parent and Nonparent Husbands and Wives." *Journal of Family Psychology* 6, no. 3 (1993): 255–265.

Leder, J. M. *Brothers and Sisters: How They Shape Our Lives.* New York: St. Martin's Press, 1991.

Lehrer, J. "DON'T! The Secret of Self-Control." *The New Yorker,* May 2009.

Levin, D., and J. Kilbourne. *So Sexy So Soon.* New York: Ballantine Books, 2008.

Levine, M. *A Mind at a Time.* New York: Simon & Schuster, 2002.

———. *The Price of Privilege.* New York: Harper, 2006.

Louv, Richard. *Last Child in the Woods: Saving Our Children from Nature-Deficit Disorder.* Chapel Hill, NC: Algonquin Books, 2005.

Marion, M. *Guidance of Young Children.* Upper Saddle River, NJ: Merrill, 1995.

Mercogliano, C. *In Defense of Childhood: Protecting Kids' Inner Wildness.* Boston: Beacon Press, 2007.

Parasuraman, S., and J. H. Greenhaus. *Integrating Work and Family: Challenges and Choices for a Changing World.* Westport, CT: Quorum Books, 1997.

Pink, David. *Drive.* New York: Riverhead, 2009.

Pipher, M. *The Shelter of Each Other: Rebuilding Our Families.* New York: Putnam Books, 1996.

Pollack, W. *Real Boys.* New York: Henry Holt, 1998.

Powers, J. *Parent-Friendly Early Learning: Tips and Strategies for Working Well with Families.* St. Paul, MN: Redleaf Press, 2005.

Pytel, B. "No More Classroom Chairs: Students Are Sitting on Exercise Balls." *Student Health Issues,* November 21, 2007.

Risman, B. J., and D. Johnson-Sumerford. "Doing It Fairly: A Study of Postgender Marriages." *Journal of Marriage and the Family* 60 (1998).

Samalin, N., and C. Whitney. *Loving Each One Best: A Caring and Practical Approach to Raising Siblings.* New York: Bantam Books, 1996.

Satter, E. *How to Get Your Child to Eat . . . But Not Too Much.* Boulder, CO: Bull Publishing, 1987.

Sax, L. *Why Gender Matters: What Parents and Teachers Need to Know About the Emerging Science of Sex Differences.* New York: Broadway Books, 2005.

_____. *Boys Adrift: The Five Factors Driving the Growing Epidemic of Unmotivated Boys and Underachieving Young Men.* New York: Basic Books, 2007.

_____. *Girls on the Edge: The Four Factors Driving the New Crisis for Girls.* New York: Basic Books, 2010.

Schilling, D. L., K. Washington, F. F. Billingsley, and J. Deitz. "Classroom Seating for Children with ADHD: Therapy Balls Versus Chairs." *American Journal of Occupational Therapy* 57, no. 5 (September/October 2003): 534–541.

Shafer, D. R. *Social and Personality Development.* Pacific Grove, CA: Brooks/Cole, 1994.

Shaw, R., with S. Wood. *The Epidemic: The Rot of American Culture, Absentee and Permissive Parenting, and the Resultant Plague of Joyless, Selfish Children.* New York: Regan Books, 2003.

Skenazy, L. "Why I Let My 9-Year-Old Ride the Subway Alone." *The Sun,* April 2008.

_____. *Free-Range Kids: Giving Our Children Freedom We Had Without Going Nuts with Worry.* San Francisco: Jossey-Bass, 2009.

Skolnick, A. S., and J. H. Skolnick. *Family in Transition.* New York: Longman, 1997.

Sroufe, L. A., R. G. Cooper, and G. B. DeHart. *Child Development: Its Nature and Course.* New York: McGraw-Hill, 1992.

Strong, B., C. DeVault, and B. W. Sayad. *The Marriage and Family Experience: Intimate Relationships in a Changing Society.* Belmont, CA: Wadsworth Publishing, 1998.

Vanzetti, N., and S. Duck. *A Lifetime of Relationships.* New York: Brooks/Cole, 1996.

Walsh, David. *No: Why Kids Need to Hear It and Ways Parents Can Say It.* New York: Free Press, 2007.

Wicks-Nelson, R., and A. C. Israel. *Behavior Disorders of Childhood*. Upper Saddle River, NJ: Prentice Hall, 1997.

Winseman, A. L., D. O. Clifton, and C. Liesveld. *Living Your Strengths.* New York: Gallup Press, 2008.

Zigler, E. F., and M. Finn Stevenson. *Children in a Changing World: Development and Social Issues.* Pacific Grove, CA: Brooks/Cole, 1993.

INDEX

Note: *f* represents a figure and *t* represents a table.

ABOUT THE AUTHOR

Jenny Hanlon is a respected teacher and consultant in the Twin Cities. She has degrees in Child Psychology and Family Education, and is licensed in early childhood education and family education. She has been working with children and families in a variety of settings since 1996.

Early in her career, Jenny was one of the founding teachers at Dodge Nature Preschool in West Saint Paul, Minnesota. She taught preschool-aged children, led parent workshops, and was the Assistant Director of the school for four years.

Jenny currently teaches parent-child classes and is the Summer Program Director at The Children's Farm School in Lake Elmo, Minnesota. Jenny is a regular contributor as a 'Parenting Expert' on a local Twin Cities talk show. She is an active volunteer and fundraiser for FamilyMeans, a nonprofit service organization.

Since 2009, Jenny has worked as a consultant for parents and professionals who work with children from birth through the early teen years. She is available for speaking engagements, parenting consultations and consulting for organizations that provide programming for children. Please visit her website at **www.jennyhanlonconsulting.com**